A NEW VOICE FOR A BROKEN SOUL

Paul A. Ray

JOSEPH KARL
PUBLISHING

Editor, Nancy Carabio Belanger, Harvey House Publishing.

Cover Design by Roseann Nieman, Niemanart Graphics,

www.niemanartgraphics.com

Book design and layout by Erin Howarth, www.wildernessbooks.org

"Not I" from Demon Hunter. 2005. *The Triptych.* Solid State Records.

To order additional copies, please contact:

Joseph Karl Publishing

P.O. Box 80371

Rochester, MI 48308

or visit

www.josephkarlpublishing.com

Library of Congress Cataloging-in-Publication Data
Ray, Paul, 1977-
    A new voice for a broken soul / By Paul Ray. -- 1st ed.
      p. cm.
    ISBN 978-1-935356-21-9
    1. Ray, Paul, 1977- 2. Catholic converts--United States--Biography. 3. Alcoholics--United States--Biography. I. Title.
    BX4668.R39A3 2012
    282.092--dc23
    [B]
                                            2012025511

Manufactured in the United States of America

Not I; I won't conform to what I see in you.

Not I; I won't surrender what I am.

Not I; and even if it was a part of me.

Not I; I'll never be that way again.

-Ryan Clark

DEMON HUNTER

Cover Photo Explanation

The cover photo represents, in part, a vision I had during my healing, which I describe in this book. It represents the altar where the Holy Sacrifice of the Mass takes place. It is where the power of this sacrament replaced the power that alcohol had in my life, as represented by the shattered glass scattered about, both on the altar itself and in the water. A flower blossoms out of a broken bottle showing a new life now illuminated by the Light of Christ beaming down. The vastness beyond the scene represents the solitude and darkness* of the road ahead in this life—only now having a destination led by the River of Life. (Revelation 22:1).

* Note: To be clear, the darkness referred to represents the darkness of the soul striving to achieve union with God—not darkness in the sense of evil.

*I dedicate this book to all people who suffer from alcohol or drug addictions. There is **always** hope through Jesus Christ! Do not be afraid to let go and let Him in!*

Contents

Introduction

I have always believed that when we can look back on our lives and see the hand of God moving we can better understand, discern, and follow Him in the future. There will always be three days in my life that I will never forget.

These are the days on which I clearly saw the hand of God Almighty at work in the most profound ways in my own life; they mark the most important events that have shaped the very sum of my existence thus far.

All of us, whether you are a beggar in the broken-down slums of a war-torn nation or the CEO of a multi-billion dollar company, were created in the very image and likeness of God (Genesis 1:26) in order that we might know, love and serve Him. This is the very end for which all of us were created. This is why we exist. [Day One: October 26, 1977] I was born into this world.

By an act of sheer grace God saw that I was not living a lifestyle that had this as my primary goal; no, far from it. He, therefore, stretched forth His mighty arm and intervened in a most miraculous way and set me back on a firm foundation. [Day Two: June 9, 2002] My miraculous deliverance.

A foundation, however, is simply a foundation and must be built upon. Subsequently, the Divine Architect labored for roughly six years laying brick after brick until He finished my new home. I officially took residence in my new abode [Day Three: April 3, 2010] I was confirmed into the Catholic Church and can now live out that which I was created for in the manner in which my Creator intended.

Foreword

This book is **not** an apologetics book. My desire is not to pit the doctrines of Catholicism and Protestantism against one another but to give a detailed description of how I arrived at Catholicism personally. In doing so, it was necessary for me to include some aspects of apologetics in order to explain to the reader the way in which God revealed the harder teachings of Catholicism to me.

The first portion of my book reviews my miraculous path from alcohol addiction to the moment when Jesus Christ, in His unfathomable mercy, healed me and delivered me from its stronghold. I will attempt to describe the horror of addiction as I knew it. I will not go into great detail concerning specific events that took place while I was drinking but stick to the essentials matters which are more conducive to the theme of the story.

The second portion of my story relates how and probably more importantly "why" our Lord Jesus Christ led me to the most misunderstood, most attacked, and most rejected religious body on earth. A journey from being the "poster child" of Protestantism, and the testimony of God's healing power through them, to the Roman Catholic Church. This book is simply an explanation of the events that took place that led me to the Catholic Church.

Like just nearly all converts who have made the journey from Protestantism to Catholicism, I never dreamed I would end up here. Humanly speaking, it would look like a ridiculous decision. After all, look at all of the scandals. Look at the abuses past and present. One could even use the very lives of so-called professing Catholics in general to further their cause as to why my choice might be deemed delirious. Why would anyone, someone might argue, walk away from the splendor of God's mercy I found myself in when I was healed in a Christian community in which the hand of God was clearly at work, and enter into something so seemingly dark and cold...so lifeless?

I am here to testify that my walk with Christ when becoming Catholic was set on fire by the Spirit of the Living God more so than I have ever had in my entire life! I have entered into the fullness of all that Christ wanted me to have! It is the very fullness He desires all His children to have.

"Qui habet aures audiendi, audiat."

"Whoever has ears to hear ought to hear."
(Matthew 11:15; 13:9; 13:43; Mark 4:9; 4:23; 7:16; Luke 8:8; 14:35)

1

Formation and Foundation

O Redeemer of my soul.

You knew me before I was born.

You knew me before the very foundation of the world.

Have pity on me as I ignored You in my youth.

Show forth Your kindness and lift me on high.

Have mercy on my wayward behavior,

And show me my own nothingness.

I've never written anything lengthy before. I haven't even taken any classes on writing. The only writing I know how to do is from what I've seen and from what I've read. And trust me—I do a lot of reading! This is not an autobiography. I will present to the reader as accurately as possible a portrait of God's overabundant mercy as I know and felt it. This is a testimony of the power of the blood of Jesus Christ, a sign of His mercy and love, and a real story about a real person. No bells, no whistles; just a prayer that this might one day do someone some good.

The mystery of God is just that—a mystery. As Christians, most of us find it difficult to determine or discern what God is doing or going to do in our lives. It's the burning question on the minds of all faithful Christians. It determines where we are and where we are headed. It's the pathway we're all called to walk; we just need to find the pathway and then follow Jesus' footsteps. I write to you my experience on how I found this road. I wasn't necessarily searching for it, nor was I really even thinking of it. It found me and brought me to Itself.

As all stories about our lives begin, I'll start my own the same way. I was born in the suburbs of Detroit, Michigan on a cool autumn morning on October 26, 1977. At this time my parents already had their hands full with two little girls. I was told that my mother's pregnancy wasn't planned and that I was a result of faulty birth control—as were a lot of babies of that time period, I presume. Regardless, my father was brought up in the old Catholic parish where my grandmother made him attend as a child. He recalls the Holy Mass being said in Latin and him not being able to determine what the priest was saying. He never spoke about his faith, however. He went to Holy Mass every Sunday and simply kept to himself the rest of the time.

My mother, on the other hand, was brought up Lutheran in the Upper Peninsula of Michigan, where the majority of "Yoopers" are Lutheran, because of their Scandinavian ancestry. I gathered that my parents weren't really serious about their faith until my birth. Yes, they went to church on Sunday but the parties and drinking told a different story. I knew something didn't line up, but never thought too much about it. I did what I was told and went to church with my mother. My parents decided that my mom should take us kids to the Lutheran church. From what I've gathered my mom took her faith more seriously than my dad, and to this day I do believe she knew God since childhood. My father went to church simply out of obligation. Apparently he never took the time to look into it further, and still cannot even explain why he does the things he does as a Catholic. This behavior prompted me later on down the road to investigate for myself why this was. It was common not only in my own family but also within every Catholic I knew at the time.

We went to the Lutheran church with our mother every week, starting as infants (we were all baptized as infants as well), and went through Sunday school and catechism. During these times I did learn a lot about Jesus, God, and the Bible. However, it didn't really take hold of me. It was still like going to school. I had to do it because my mom insisted, yet I didn't protest until later on. My memories of church, Sunday school, and catechism are limited. I can recall different aspects and different things we did but never a real encounter with God in the sense that I left with a feeling of complete truthfulness. I made my first communion when I was in the 6th grade. Still, after this there were times of joy but it was never complete. I never opened myself up enough to allow the Holy Spirit to work in me. I didn't know how nor did I really even know that He could. We were taught the tenets of the faith, but the relationship aspect was either left out or I wasn't paying attention and/or inviting it. After I turned 18 years old my mom gave me the choice of whether or not I wanted to continue to go to church. So, naturally, I didn't go every week, just every so often.

During this time I really "broadened my horizons" so to speak. I didn't take my faith seriously and didn't really think of it at all except on certain occasions. I wasn't against it but more or less had the notion that "If it works for you then more power to you; it's just not my thing." I went through middle school and then high school and drew even further away from church and God. By this time it was just a memory of something I "graduated" from, and no longer had its weight to hold me down. I began to explore the REAL world.

I began working at a small local grocery store and became very close to my coworkers, most of whom were already my friends. We started hanging out and going to parties. It was the "experimental phase" of my life. I'll never forget the first time I drank alcohol and actually got drunk. My friend and I planned on stealing a 40-ounce bottle of beer from the grocery store where we worked and planned on meeting up later that night to share it. We agreed on meeting at midnight or around 1 A.M.—the time when we both knew the rest of our families were going to be asleep. Well, I snuck out of the house and went to his; he only lived a few houses down from me so I wasn't driving. Much to my surprise, he had fallen asleep! So I took the bottle myself and went back home and drank it in my basement alone. I'll never forget the euphoria it gave me. The first sensation of being drunk was unlike any other feeling I'd had before. I knew I was going to like this! The actual taste wasn't the greatest, but once the alcohol took its natural effect it didn't bother me. I spent the remainder of the night listening to music and basking in this newfound ecstasy.

Once the day had ended and morning came, I couldn't wait to tell my friends of this experience! This, of course, only reinforced bad behavior and was the beginning of a downward spiral. But being young, youth's rebellion was in the air and better things seemed just beyond the horizon.

As time went on we began to steal more and more alcohol, find people who were of legal age to buy it for us, or drive down to different parts of the inner city where they didn't check ID. Week after week we'd find a party and just party the night away. Whether it was at someone's house, in a park, or anywhere, we thought we could get away with drinking. This was living the high life for a 17-year-old guy. I felt as if I were on top of the world! I never spent time chasing after women or getting into fights. I would simply socialize and relax, have a good time. Feeling as if

I were an adult and could "hold my liquor" was the one thing I needed to boost my self-confidence.

Even though I did not realize it at the time, there was a deeper reason to why I turned to alcohol. One could say that alcoholism ran in my genes; that it was inherited. After all, a very large portion of my extended family drank. However, the roots of my own alcoholism extend even deeper than that. It took a lot of praying and understanding about myself in light of who I am and who I always was, a child of the Living God made in His image and likeness, to figure out the genesis of why I drank. The euphoria from the intoxication was a boost to my otherwise shy demeanor. I was more outgoing and I felt I could act genuinely with those around me because of it. Alcohol gave me the ability to be who I wanted to be. This creates dependency and dependency is addiction. My heart was yearning to be loved. Since, therefore, alcohol gave me a boost of self-confidence I felt that it was through this perception of being able to be more outgoing that more people would take notice and I would essentially feel the love for which my heart longed. Alcohol, I felt, gave me the ability to "put myself out there" and be noticed. I felt I had to earn the love of those around me.

Subsequently, I found myself held in the clutches of alcohol more than my friends. Within a year or so I began to drink just about every day while my friends stuck with the weekends only. Because of this, I had to find ways to buy booze outside of the help of my friends. From the age of about 18 until 21, I drove down to one of the worst parts of Detroit to buy three 40-ounce bottles of (oddly enough) St. Ides Malt Liquor. I even became good friends with the guys who worked down there; even some of the locals recognized me and would stop to talk. It must have been by God's sheer grace that after hundreds of times going down there I never once ran into trouble.

I was living it up! I had my drinks and I had everything a teenage man could want from the world. I had a car, a job, and what made matters even better was that I had the opportunity to move out of my parents' house. Before long I began hanging out with friends who were over 21. This made getting alcohol a little easier. I simply gave them the money, told them what I wanted, and they would buy it for me. This happened on a daily basis. If they weren't around I would simply drive to Detroit myself and take care of my needs that way. By this time I was working at a car wash and there were some slow days due to bad weather. So to fill in the gaps my buddies and I would buy alcohol before (and sometimes during) work and consume it while working. We got our job done and we somehow were able to work well with drinking and working. No one got absolutely loaded to the point where they would literally stumble. Well, only once or twice, but we quickly learned our lesson.

What should've been a real eye-opener for me was when I was a junior in high school. A friend of mine had a fake ID. He looked identical to his 23-year-old brother, so he used his brother's ID to buy alcohol. He and I would spend many days drinking together. The problem was that we never had anywhere "safe" where we could drink. We couldn't go to our own houses because our parents would be home, and we couldn't go to the bar because of our age. So one day we decided to just stay in the car and finish off our 12-pack. Did I mention that it was in a school parking lot? Despite the parking lot being empty, because it was after school hours, someone told on us and the police came. My friend got his car impounded and we both got a ticket for being minors consuming alcohol on school property. Strange how we didn't get arrested or even taken into the police station and having our parents called.

You would think that an event like this would sober one up, but not me. A couple years later a bunch of us went over to a work friend's house for a party. It lasted into the small hours of the morning. Then I still had to get home. It was about a 20-minute drive back to my house, and I agreed that I would follow my friend home just to see that he got home safe, because he had had more to drink than I did. We were just about home when I saw a police car coming the other direction. Without thinking, I panicked and decided to make a sharp turn down a side street to avoid any contact with him. Bad move. He ended up doing a U-turn and following me about halfway down the side street before he pulled me over. To make a long story short, at age 18, I was arrested for drunk driving.

I had to spend some time in jail and was completely humiliated. Not to mention the thousands of dollars that my parents had to pay in fines and court costs. When I think back on this event, it would be sufficient to say that it should have been the wake-up call to my drinking, but unfortunately it wasn't. I was ignoring all of the warning signs. Despite the immensity of the situation, my addiction was stronger.

It is interesting to note here the hand of almighty God. For the better part of three years I ran into very little trouble. Yes, I now had a DUI on my record, but to be honest it should've been far worse. I drank and drove literally every day. I had been pulled over while drinking on a couple of occasions but was let go for whatever reason. I drove into some of the worst parts of the city of Detroit to purchase alcohol hundreds of times and never once ran into any problem. I marvel at God's kindness to my own stupidity.

I was still in high school during some of this time. I would sometimes drink before school and also during lunch hour. Every day found me planning around how I was able to get drunk—figuring out the whens and wheres of how I could satisfy this longing for being intoxicated. At this time, most of my friends didn't know how much I actually drank. I was beginning to get careless. My life was violently spinning out of control and I, nor anyone else, could stop me.

I always keep these truths firmly planted in my mind and heart, and remind myself always of His mercy and grace during these times. He only knows what would have happened to me had He not protected me the way He did. Glory be to the Father, and to the Son and to the Holy Spirit, as it was in the beginning, is now and ever shall be, world without end. AMEN.

2

I'm Broken:
The Descent into the Abyss

Most merciful, heavenly Father,

You watched as I fell,

My life spoke of the wretchedness of the

fallen human nature.

My heart cried out for love but I sought it

Where it was not.

The whole while all I longed for was You,

But I didn't know it.

The time came when I was going to turn 21 years old. I was relieved in a way, but part of me felt as if it wasn't such a big ordeal. Yes, I could now buy alcohol from the corner store instead of having to drive to Detroit, stealing it, or having someone else buy for me. I spent my 21st birthday alone in my basement. No bells and whistles. I legally bought my first bottle of liquor—a fifth of Jim Beam Whiskey, which would soon become my drink of choice. From my 21st birthday on I consumed mostly hard liquor, every day. It tasted awful but it got the job done quicker. Before work I would stop at the corner store and buy a pint of J.B. and pour it into my Coke bottle and sip on it throughout the day. After work I would stop at the liquor store again and buy a liter of J.B. I'd finish most of it before night's end and save the rest for the next day and then repeat the process. This went on every single day for about three years.

It became such a habit that I couldn't imagine my life without it. In fact, the odd thing is it felt as if I were "drunk" when I was actually sober. I was the type who could drink a bottle of whiskey and it would hardly show—at least at first. My tolerance skyrocketed and I soon learned that I needed more and more alcohol to achieve the same effects. But, at this point in my life, I needed alcohol simply to survive.

One day I had to go to the Secretary of State office to renew my driver's license, which I found very ironic because it allowed me to continue to drive drunk. When I woke up I decided that I wouldn't drink until I got home, for obvious reasons. However, as we all probably know, when at the Secretary of State or DMV office we have to wait in line quite a bit, sometimes for hours. I had underestimated my withdrawals, and while waiting for my turn I had a panic attack the likes of which I never known. I began to shake like a leaf and became very nauseous. When my number was called, I nervously walked up to the counter and immediately the clerk asked if I was all right and if I had been on any medication. I couldn't even look into machine which tests for visual acuity because I was trembling so badly. She then told me to take a seat and come back to the counter when I was ready. All eyes were on me, as I was a spectacle to behold. How terrible it was! The stares from the other people were like lasers piercing me with jeers of utter disgrace and shame. I'm pretty sure the devil had a field day at this!

Eventually I regained my composure (by the grace of God) and got out of there with a renewed license, which would only serve to put other people's lives, and my own, in jeopardy. Once I got home I got hammered immediately and tried to put this unfortunate and shameful event behind me. Little did I know that this single event would haunt me for years to come, only to be outdone by the strength of almighty God in time and trust.

As my consumption of alcohol increased, I began to experience its side effects in a real way—not only in my relationships with the people around me and with my job, but also concerning my own health. I never ate as I should; therefore, I did not receive all of the essential vitamins and nutrients I needed to stay healthy. My body began to slowly shut itself down. I would experience increasing numbness in my limbs and sharp pains in my side. I simply ignored them and continued to drink. After all, it created a perception of false reality in more ways than one. I didn't want to face the reality that my body was beginning to shut itself down. When others my age were in the so-called prime of their lives, I was withering away. Whenever an addiction is of this magnitude, one is simply blinded to reality. It's present and obvious to everyone around them but the stronghold of the addiction itself is more overpowering to the one addicted than the realities around them are. At least to me, I knew it existed but I didn't want to face it. I was afraid to face it because these destructive actions had become such a vital part of my life—a deadly part, but nevertheless a real one.

It got to the point where everyday chores were difficult. A simple thing such as walking up a flight of stairs now became very tiresome and trivial. I always had shortness of breath. I was weak and had to move slowly because anything more required far too much effort than I had to give. I was continuously out of energy and nothing mattered to me except feeding my addiction. It seemed to me it was the only thing in my life that mattered. I could not stop drinking even if I had desired to. I even tried to quit cold turkey, but I quickly learned that the withdrawals alone would have killed me. Every single morning I would wake up shaking and wanting more, completely terrified of my life. Alcohol was my medicine; ironically, it was the remedy that kept me motivated. I had to drink at all hours of being awake. It was the first thing I did upon getting up and the last thing I did before retiring to bed. The first sip of the morning was always the hardest to swallow. The mere smell made me gag, let alone the taste. But it was something I knew I had to do if I wanted to function. I would oftentimes cough up what I just swallowed and vomit blood—sometimes violently. My throat was parched and continually on fire; my side was always aching. But I had to have that first drink or else I was a nervous wreck. Or worse: I'd die.

I want to pause here and ask the reader to think about what I've just said. Try to understand the state in which addicts find themselves. Under the most horrific conditions they continue to feed the very habit that they realize is killing them. Human nature itself has a God-given yearning to live, and it fights to stay alive. In my own experience I marvel at how much violence my body took upon itself before it started to give up. It doesn't matter what someone is addicted to—the result remains the same. It always leads to death. Even if we do not want death (and who in his right mind does) and try to avoid it, we see that through an addiction we are completely powerless against it. The consequences of being enslaved to anything cannot be undone by human hands even though the enslavement was brought about by those same hands. This is that nature of sin. I experienced this first hand, and cannot describe the utter helplessness I felt.

Oddly enough, however, I was still working almost every day. My same old routine hadn't lessened, but in a way it increased because of my decaying addiction. I had to work to get the money in order to provide for my addiction. I was walking into work one afternoon after mixing my usual alcoholic concoction when I lost my balance and fell face first onto the ground in front of all my coworkers, the customers, and the owner of the company. He witnessed the entire event unfold and called me into his office. He then proceeded to explain to me that he was aware of my condition and advised me to take the day off. At the time, I didn't have a car so I had to call a friend and have him come pick me up. Needless to say I was humiliated. That was the bottom of the barrel, so to speak, at least up to that point.

After that, I never returned to work. I didn't want to face my coworkers anymore, nor did I have the desire, strength, or will to work anymore. I was tired, weak, and out of control; something had to give. I felt myself and my life spinning downward into hell, but there wasn't anything I could do about it. My family and friends all knew of this huge elephant in the room, but no one said anything about it. I realize the position I put everyone in and felt just awful about it. I needed help but I didn't want it—I was terrified of seeking it. I was bound in chains to an addiction much stronger than I realized, and there was no way out of it, no person to help, and no hope left. Did I seek pity? Probably, but I knew I did this to myself. Why, I thought, would anyone pity me since it was by my own stupidity that I ended up in this most horrific situation? I didn't deserve pity at all, and the realization of this caused me even more sorrow and sunk me down into an even deeper pit of despair. All I wanted the whole time was love.

As a result, I found myself without a job, no source of income, and an addiction to alcohol. It was my own dead end. I therefore had to move back home with my parents. Luckily I had a roof over my head. But other than that I was alone. I still had to tend to my addiction but had no money to do so. I would resort to stealing money or the alcohol any way I could. God knows how fortunate I was to never get caught. I would drink my parents' alcohol as well, to the point where they had to lock it up.

Having an addiction causes people to do things they know are wrong. They cannot help it because their addiction is far stronger than their conscience telling them that what they're doing is wrong. It literally doesn't matter what extremes need to be taken in order to fulfill that which they believe they need. In this state of mind the addicted individual is very dangerous; not only to themselves but to those around them. Speaking for myself, I knew I didn't want to harm anybody but the addiction within me forced me to not care if I did. I did things, without even thinking, that I will never soon forget.

On top of this miserable existence I created for myself, my health was deteriorating quickly. On one occasion I recall having a ministroke. I had just stepped out of the shower when I began to shake uncontrollably. My right arm went numb and my vision blurred. My heart was racing as I quickly got dressed, made it to my bedroom, threw open the window, and lay down in hopes that it would pass. It was winter at the time and the air was freezing but I was burning. Within an hour I poured my first drink and the "deathrattle shakes" ceased. Panic was an everyday phenomenon. Every hour of every day my focus was on alcohol. How do I get it, where can I drink it, and how much will I drink. My life was completely centered around alcohol to the point where nothing else mattered. My family, my job, and even my own life didn't mean a single thing to me. There was no escaping this either. I would wake up in the morning thinking about it and go to bed at night dreading the next day. I can even recall the morning of September 11, 2001. I was extremely hung over—as usual—when my mom woke me up to tell me the twin towers had been bombed. I got up and watched the events unfold for a bit and went back to bed hoping and praying that this was the end of the world. I needed anything, at this point, to take the focus away from me. Sadly, it took something as horrific as the September 11th bombings to do so. And even this, as time would have it, made matters worse for me.

I was so self-absorbed; I had no love in my heart. I was constantly in sorrow, anger, hurt, and misery. Pitiable and wretched, I licked my wounds and simply waited to die. I lost all hope in myself, in the people around me, and in God—if He even cared. What would become of me but death deserved?

It had gotten harder and harder to drink, especially the very first drink of the day. I had reached the point where I usually ended up vomiting the first drink until my body finally accepted the alcohol. There was simply no way around it. Life was overwhelming. The darkness was overpowering. The entrapment I was in held me and would not let go no matter how hard I tried to resist it. I knew I had to quit but I also knew that it was impossible. The constant struggle of finding a way to get drunk every single day wears a person out. It was all that I did on a day-to-day basis and I was paying for it greatly. I wasn't eating, I could hardly walk, and I always hurt physically. I looked like the walking dead. My skin was gray and the whites of my eyes were as the color of apple juice (a sign of a bad liver), and I was weak. I had absolutely no consolation at all.

Couple this with the constant jeers of those who knew me, who would always state the obvious. "You know you're killing yourself." I knew full well that I was dying. I didn't want to accept this fact, but nevertheless, it was true. I was forced to accept it by default, and this brought me unspeakable pain and agony.

Even though I knew I was dying, I didn't want to. I knew that if I died, I would end up in even worse shape—suffering in hell. I was scared out of my wits. If you will, try to envision yourself in this situation. It is as if you have no way out; the inevitable destination is suicide. It is only a matter of how you will do it.

I clearly remember times sitting alone drinking in utter misery, telling myself, "This isn't me." I would reflect back on my childhood and wonder what happened. I looked back at a time of innocence and wept in self-pity. I wondered why I made these horrible choices. My friends were all moving on in their lives, and I was moving nowhere. The shame and the humiliation of the whole circumstance were overwhelming—I lived in constant fear and anxiety. Even sleeping brought no relief. I had horrific night terrors. My hell had begun already, and there was no way around it. Everything was soaked in black, inside and out. No hope, no relief in sight, and death constantly following me. I lived a life of solitude and abandonment from the world. I didn't want anyone to see me in this state. I was helpless and alone.

"Almighty God, Father, Son, and Holy Spirit.

You allowed me a glimpse of hell.

By my own undoing I freely fled Your protection.

My soul in anguish, my heart defeated.

You watched as I lost everything.

Yet, in Your unfailing compassion,

You did not forsake me."

I knew I needed help, and fast, but I was absolutely scared to death to seek that help, because I didn't want to give up drinking. Not only that, but I knew that rehab would mean having to leave home for a while, and the thought of having to fight against the withdrawals with strangers was something I did not want to face. All of this plus the sheer humiliation factor terrified me. I just wanted it to be like the days when I first started to drink. Things

16

were fun and I always recovered. But I knew that wasn't going to happen. My mom, in obvious distress, forced me to see a doctor because of my physical ailments. My limbs were numb and I had no balance whatsoever, and my side (my liver) was throbbing most of the time. The pain and unsightliness were unavoidable, and as a result I had no choice but to go. So the day came and I went to see the family physician. He was rather brief with me. He took some blood samples and told me that I had an enlarged liver—without even examining me! A few days later, the results of the blood samples came in, and the only thing that he told me was a resounding, "You MUST stop drinking!" No help, no advice, just an impossible command. He also referred me to a gastrointestinal doctor. Upon visiting with him I had to get some pretty invasive tests run on me in the hospital concerning the pains in my side. The entire ordeal was surreal. This wasn't happening to me; it couldn't be. I was so young—just 23—and my whole life was ahead of me. While all my peers were moving ahead in their lives, I was moving backwards. Having to go through all of these tests was an absolute embarrassment.

When I went back a week or so later to get the results from the gastrointestinal doctor, he sat both my mother and me down before even reading to us the results and said:

"Paul, you have one foot in the gutter and one foot in the grave. I refuse to help you until you yourself get some help with your drinking. At the rate that you're drinking, you probably only have six months to one year left to live."

This news could probably have been predicted; however, hearing it from a third party just brought it to fruition. It was real. Never before in our family had anything of this magnitude reared its ugly head. Never before in most families has anything like this ever occurred! It won't come as a surprise to say that the drive home was silent.

17

The days following my doctor visits are a blur. Even looking back, I cannot remember anything but despair; all hope was lost. I was at my worst. I had no money and an addiction that I could not break for the life of me—literally. I was desperate. I knew I couldn't stop drinking and everyone else knew it too. What do you say to someone in this condition? I can only imagine my family's thoughts at a time like this. I was in the very depths of darkness. In the clutches of the devil and I didn't know it. Spiritually speaking, I was being dragged into hell and I was to blame. I couldn't point fingers. I couldn't blame anyone else but myself for the miserable state I found myself in. All I wanted was to die, but at the same time, I knew that had I died I would end up in a far worse place than what I was in.

Every day was spent alone. I was unwanted and left for dead. Nor did I feel like talking to anyone. What was there to say? I simply awaited death by myself. I was convinced that getting help wasn't even an option; I was too far gone. Each day was unbearable. The mental and physical anguish I was in was begging for relief but none came. I gave up on life completely. I surrendered.

Around this time I was going through the radio stations late one night and happened across a radio show that featured a minister who did nothing else but take calls for prayer requests and pray for these people on the air. I got bold and called in. I explained to him that my sister was getting married in a couple of weeks and I knew that I would be face to face with the reality that I wouldn't be able to drink at will. I was terrified at the thought of not only facing my family but with the withdrawals that come with not being able to drink. I knew that my extended family would be in attendance and there was no way of hiding my condition. The physical damage was evident and by just looking at me one could figure out that something was seriously wrong with me. So, after describing all of this to the minister, he prayed for me. This was the first time

I can recall reaching out to God. Before this, I felt as if God had given up on me. I felt that all hope was gone. To this day, I am extremely thankful for this step, as I truly believe it paved the way for where I am today.

So the time arrived when my sister was getting married. Things weren't all that bad at first. The wedding itself was on beautiful and historic Mackinac Island, and not having been there in a long while brought with it a somewhat serene atmosphere. The day before the wedding, we were all having dinner at a fancy restaurant on the island when my aunt sparked a conversation with me. My aunt is the mother of my cousin whom I spent some time living with. He had the same addictions as I did and sought help about a year or so before. He was waiting for his release from a rehab facility in a week or so after the wedding, and my aunt asked me if I would be interested in visiting him. I agreed. She also reminded me of God's mercy and loving kindness, to which I agreed, but I didn't think much about it. Having the thought that God was upset with me— and the thought of "religion" in general—just wasn't my thing. She was the first person to actually witness to me about the love of Christ in my weakened state. I am forever grateful for her example.

When the day of the wedding was upon us, I actually felt pretty good despite trying to mask the withdrawals I was hav- ing. The reception was typical: an open bar and everyone having a good time. Everyone knew of my condition and no one said anything. So I made my way to the bar and began to drink. Of course one led to another, and I was beginning to feel "normal." It was then that my other sister took notice and mentioned that if I were to drink I had better see if the bride (my sister) minded. So I asked, thinking she would be all right with it because a wed- ding is a once-in-a-lifetime event. Well, she did mind, and told me that she would rather not have me drink. At this point, out of respect for my sister, I stopped. I left the reception and thought that my whole world had just collapsed all around me. Everyone was happily enjoying the festivities and I couldn't. After all, it was my own fault for getting into this predicament. It was at this point that thoughts of suicide actually crept in. I felt hopeless and abandoned. I thought, why would anyone take something away from me that made me happy? A completely selfish motive, but at the time it was all I had. I wept bitterly and took a long walk by myself until the wee hours of the morning.

3

A Light in the Darkness

O my Savior!

Amidst the mire I made of my life You had a plan.

You reached out in mercy

And embraced me when I did not deserve it.

How, then, can I ever adequately thank You?

A week or so after my sister's wedding, my aunt followed through with the invitation for me to visit my now-rehabilitated cousin. I had nothing to lose. I knew I was dying and at this point I didn't care. I was ashamed and perhaps I simply wanted something different to do. No one could possibly understand what I was going through unless they themselves had been there, so I thought a visit to my cousin might help shed a little light. Little did I know what was in store!

My aunt came to pick me up, and at the time I was a nervous wreck; I hadn't had any alcohol in my system and the withdrawals where manifesting themselves. I had tried to search for some extra booze that I may have left in one of the many bottles I had laying around before I knew I was going to be picked up. I didn't know what to expect but I was open to almost anything, I had to be, because I had nowhere else to turn. I figured this was an attempt by my family to try and convince me to go into rehab, something I knew that I did not want to do. The mere thought of it was humiliating and horrific. Nevertheless, it had been a very long time since I actually went anywhere sober. I didn't want to go without at least having some alcohol in my system. My attempts, however, were unsuccessful, so by the time my aunt arrived to pick me up, I was bone-dry sober and paying for it!

As we were driving, a song came on that I had never heard before. I hadn't known any other Christian music besides the hymns from growing up in the Lutheran church. This song was different, however, and it sparked something within me that I never knew I had—a heart. The song was called, "I Can Only Imagine." As the song played, I felt myself "melting" inside. I couldn't hold back the tears even though I had no idea what was happening. I had glimpses or flashbacks at what I had gotten myself into in my life, and somehow I knew that there was hope. I remembered the innocence of my childhood and longed for it again. But I couldn't put all the pieces together just yet. I didn't know what this meant. There was a churning inside of me. Something (or someone) was attempting to soften my heart. I felt a feeling of comfort somewhat like the feeling a child would have while in the safety of his parents. I hid the tears as best as I could, for fear of ridicule and embarrassment, but I knew that my aunt knew. She had to know! This, of course, was the Holy Spirit reawakening my soul to revive it. It was almost beyond my control, because no matter how hard I tried to fight it, He wouldn't yield. My heart was aching. I felt as if I knew someone cared for me. In my mind I thought, "How is that possible?" Everyone had rejected me as a lost cause but this something or someone who was pulling at my heartstrings continued to penetrate my inner most being with something I never knew existed.

It was good to see my cousin. He was on fire for Christ and looking good! He related story after story of how Christ had changed him, but I could not share in his enthusiasm because my mind was still preoccupied with alcohol. I was supposed to leave that same day but was asked if I would be interested in coming along with them to church on the following day. I agreed. I hadn't been to church in a while and I had nothing against it, so I said yes. The night before, while catching up on old times, my cousin, his friend, and I were talking about different things. They expressed their enthusiasm at me being able to meet their pastor and their new church in general. My cousin said something to the effect of, "Something great is going to happen tomorrow." However, I wasn't very excited to go because I was embarrassed by my condition. I felt I really had no choice.

I hardly slept that night. I actually prayed for the first time in a long time. I recall asking God, if He wasn't angry with me, to grant me strength to follow through. I had no idea how my body would react concerning the withdrawals. So morning eventually came and we left for church. I had never been to this church before, but I noticed how different it was compared to what I was used to. There was no altar, just a stage and instruments used during praise and worship. The actual church was very small—the building looked as if it had been someone's house at one point. Upon entering, I specifically felt something—if I could be so bold as to call it that—inside of me telling, shouting rather, for me to leave. I did not want to be there. It was a force trying to keep me away, as if it knew what was going to happen. I literally felt a sensation that something BIG was about to happen, and it scared me greatly. But I went in regardless.

I was introduced and welcomed by many members of the

church, as well as the pastor, and took a seat by myself. I had no idea what to do, because I had never been to a church service like this before. It was all new to me. The church had a band and began playing different songs that I had never heard before, and people began to sing and some even danced. "What is all of this?" I asked myself. It all seemed surreal. At this point I got that "melting" feeling again, and hoped that I would not break down! What humiliation that would bring. However, I couldn't help but weep bitterly again. Only this time it lasted for what felt like an eternity. While everyone was singing and dancing, I sat down and covered my face and wept like a child. I was embarrassed yet at the same time I didn't care. It was right at this moment that I had a vision. When I say "vision" I do not mean that I saw something with my physical eyes. It was something I saw from within. I knew what I was seeing but I didn't see it naturally. In order to describe it, I need to relate a few things about me first.

I'm a huge pet lover! I absolutely love pets, especially cats and dogs. Ever since I can remember, I've always had a big heart for animals. In my vision I saw a big shaggy dog, something like a sheep dog, curled up, wet, cold, and shaking. My heart immediately went out to him. I began petting him and assuring him that everything would be all right and that I would take care of him. Suddenly, the big shaggy dog turned into a person laying in the fetal position, shaking and scared. It was me. But can you guess who was comforting me? Jesus! I knew immediately right there and then that Jesus was absolutely real and that He loved me beyond my imagination. I just knew it; I can't explain it to you but I knew it, despite my failures and addictions. He embraced me like the prodigal son. He didn't come in wrath and anger, disappointment, or judgment. He did not play the role of judge, jury, and executioner but, rather, He met me where I was with open arms and pure love! The mere thought of how someone could still love me despite all that I had done confused me. Yet it was the most real thing that has happened to me. I was swimming in true love completely beside myself. The mercy, love, and raw compassion that enveloped me was flowing directly into my heart and spilling into my entire being. It was a moment of sheer ecstasy, where I didn't even know if what was happening was really happening! O, this love of God is available to everyone! Cry out to Him for it!

Almost immediately after this, the praise and worship had finished. The pastor was about to give his sermon when he paused to speak with someone privately off to the side. He then looked directly at me and asked, "Are you Paul? Paul Ray?" I was confused as to how he knew my *full* name, so I consequently looked around me and answered, "Yes, I am." He then asked if I could come up front so that he could pray for me. I agreed. He then told me the following:

"I was just talking with one of our elders and she described to me a recent dream that she had. In her dream she said that she was at someone's funeral. She walked up to the casket and looked in and noticed the body in the casket twitch. She began to pray fervently. The body, as a result, sat up, climbed out of the casket, and walked out of the church. She then told me that when you first walked into the church today, she knew without a shadow of a doubt that the person in the casket was you!"

He proceeded to tell me all about my condition. He knew about my addiction, as if God Himself were speaking through him. He asked me if it would be all right for them to pray for me. With tears and a sense of true gratefulness, I agreed without hesitation. I didn't know what to expect. I thought briefly to myself, "Well, I'm already in this far; I might as well take it further." Despite not knowing what to expect, I believe that I knew it was the enemy's last attempt to stop this. The pastor asked if I believed that Jesus Christ could heal me. I answered with a resounding "Yes!" He started to pray…and pray…and pray, as did the entire congregation along with him. What I felt was similar to what I thought a heart attack would feel like. From my neck all the way to my waist, I felt as if my spine were on fire. A literal burning sensation coursed through me. Something was happening to me.

During this prayer, I recall another brief vision that lasted about a second or two. I saw an altar, of sorts, with empty alcohol bottles of all kinds sitting on top. Then, in a violent force, the arm of Jesus Christ swung across the top of the altar and completely shattered every bottle—thus, symbolically demolishing the stronghold of alcohol in my life. I now understood, in a profound way, His anger toward the devil's tools of bondage like alcohol and other means of addiction. It was as if I were caught up in a whirlwind and just went wherever it took me. I remember having my eyes closed as the tears never ceased to flow. All I remember sensing at this point was what seemed like waves of glory. It seemed that the power of God was passing through the entire church like waves in a lake. One wave after another crashed through us, leaving the heavens exposed and the sheer majesty of almighty God showing over us. I could tell by the sound of the prayers of the faithful and the overabundant love that coursed through my being. It was surreal. What came next was the most beautiful thing that anyone could ever experience.

As the praying concluded, the pastor said that our Lord required just one more thing for me to do. At this point I had no idea what had just occurred, but I was up for anything, I was desperate and I knew I was in the midst of something beyond my capacity. The pastor then said that Jesus wanted me to literally SHOUT the name Jesus three times as loud as I could. Can you picture this? Here I am, a shy person to begin with, having to shout at the top of my lungs in front of the entire congregation of people whom I don't even know! But I didn't care; I knew something great was happening to me, so with a firm resolve in my voice…I shouted the first JESUS!…then the second. On the third shout the most indescribable thing happened. The millisecond after I shouted the third and final JESUS I felt something leave me. A weight was immediately lifted. It was as if I were literally a new creation. I felt as though I just stepped out of a long, hot shower that cleansed both the inside and out; I was floating. And best of all, I was absolutely flooded with an overpowering, pure, undefiled love. It engulfed my entire being. I knew that I actually meant something to someone. I felt as if I were placed on a pedestal before the very angels of heaven and marveled at. The combination of these two "sensations" brought with it empowerment, strength, courage, boldness, humility, and most importantly love.

The strange thing about this entire event is that I was not even praying for deliverance. Perhaps other people were, but if we're honest with ourselves, how often does God really perform physical miracles? This singular episode in my life speaks volumes of what God has called me out to do in life. The sheer rarity and profound significance cannot be underestimated. I had but little faith and had given up on God. Nevertheless, He reached out in love even when I basically spat in His face! I was given a second chance in life and was absolutely humbled.

After the service the entire congregation surrounded me and everyone was hugging me and singing praises to the Lord our God. I can recall the word, "Glory" repeating itself over and over in my head. And the best thing, which really didn't hit me until a little later that day, was the realization that I didn't feel like drinking! My desire to drink was completely taken away! I didn't have any withdrawal symptoms or shakes. I didn't even worry about how or where I could get my next drink. Keep in mind that I hadn't felt this way for nearly five years.

The pastor himself sat behind the scene in the back of the church and just wept. He had never before been through nor even seen such a dramatic display of God's power at work. He said a while after that that what really got him was when he noticed the yellow that was in the whites of my eyes (which was due to a bad liver) disappear as he was looking at them.

4

Glory

---

*My soul will forever proclaim the majesty of
Almighty God!*

He has granted me a new life,

He broke the chains and destroyed the shackles,

Surrender has been given a new name!

The days immediately following my deliverance were indescribable. I would do myself (and God) an injustice to try and put into mere words the experience. Once I had left the church where all of this took place I felt as if I was literally floating in mid-air. I felt light. I knew without a doubt that something extraordinary had happened to me. Was I free? Did I want to drink? To be honest, if I absolutely had to describe this aspect of my healing I would liken it to stepping out of a long, hot shower after not having showered in months and after working continually in the filthiest of conditions. However, the fact stayed the same: I was freed! I knew within me that I was a new creation. I had been given something that very few people are given. In such a dramatic way at that! How would my mind, my body react? What was I to expect?

The most immediate change was the continual ringing within my mind of the words, "Glory! Glory! Glory!" Over and over again these words permeated not only my mind but in a mystical way my entire being. It was accompanied by a strange, unfamiliar light or brightness the likes of which I was not familiar with. I saw it not with my physical eyes but within my soul. A soul that, just an hour before, had not known of such brightness. I was drawn to it and it embraced me. So comforting and new was the combination of these two phenomena that I could not tell if I were dreaming. "What has happened to me?" I thought. I was so full of love that I felt that I could melt at any given moment. To this day it was truly the greatest sensation I have ever known. The longing that I had felt my whole life—to be wanted, loved and valued—was satisfied completely. Far beyond the petty, base, momentary glimpses of pleasure and satisfaction that alcohol or any other thing or person has ever given me. I had something to live for. I knew life had a meaning and that God is love!

That same day a bunch of us went out to eat after the service to a local pizza place, and for the first time in a very long time I did not desire alcohol. I wasn't even thinking about it. It never even crossed my mind! How is that? I didn't ponder this at the time because there was no need to. One thing was for sure; I ate like I never ate before! I had an appetite for the first time in years. Everything was safe. No fear whatsoever. No worrying about where my next drink would come from or if I would have enough to get me intoxicated. There simply was no need for that. It never even entered into my head. This was a new beginning for me. The notion that I could start from scratch again was too good to be true. Plus, I did not fear losing it. I never had the thought, "What if this goes away? What if God is just giving me a taste of what I *could* be like?" Even the thought of dread that my desire to drink might eventually return didn't bother me. It was completely gone. It was no longer a part of me. O, the sheer grace!

Shortly thereafter, my aunt remembered that God had given her a spiritual word concerning me; it was about three months before I was actually healed. From time to time she receives divinely inspired personal revelations concerning the will of God in her own life and sometimes in the lives of those around her, and she writes them down in order to not forget them. One evening, a few days after my deliverance, she read to me the following, which dealt with what had just happened:

(dated March 20, 2002. I was healed on June 9, 2002)

"The peace of the Lord is with you. Gather all into this peace. The calling of Paul to the altar is the matter of most importance as his life will be lost if he does not come into obedience now. He is an important part in My Kingdom but I cannot use him in his present state. As he comes forth to the promise, I will heal his physical ills and his testimony will lead many to My Kingdom. The call on his life has been confirmed; lead him to the place of rest and all will be taken from him. There is nothing in this world that he cherishes other than the Father in Heaven. His heart is ripe and for the fruit to grow he needs to be pruned to deliver the Word out, to the Father. Do not hesitate to go to him and have him receive me and I will care for all his needs. His path will be one of Godly righteousness and he will lead his family into the Kingdom."

Even to this day it gives me chills simply to read it!

I remained with my cousin and his family for most of that week. Day after day found me in a continual heavenly bliss! No withdrawals whatsoever. No desire to drink. However, despite the Lord healing my physical body of the damage that alcohol had caused, I still had to deal with my own physical weaknesses. I hadn't worked out or exercised for a long time, so my muscles were like rubber. In a word, I was weak. My sense of balance had returned, but since I wasn't used to it, I felt as if I were not balanced at all. I literally had to retrain my body to work properly. Yes, I no longer suffered the pains in my sides and the loss of feeling in my limbs, but I had to rediscover how to use them. It may sound strange to read that, but that is how bad alcohol affected my system.

I noticed over the next few weeks that my body responded very quickly to rebuilding itself to its intended, healthy state. It seemed that my body was thirsty for exercise and I slowly began to build my muscles back to normal, literally within a month. I fell in love with walking. Each day I would take advantage of my time off (I didn't have a job now for quite a few months) and just go for long walks. My dog, Speedy, came along and I'm pretty sure that he too enjoyed the new me! These long walks were very special to me. I saw God in everything now. His Holy presence was screaming from everything created, and I was soaking it all in and simply thanking Him for the opportunity to witness all of this. I felt as if Jesus Himself were at my side walking with me, like a long lost friend who has returned for good. It was very personal and I grew in my love for Him. To this day I treasure few things as I do these long walks.

I returned home some four or five days after my deliverance. I had been somewhat concerned about coming back home, because I didn't yet know how I would react to my return to the "scene of the crime," so to speak. Would I return to my old habits once I settled back into my old routine? I knew that it would be different, but as to how different, I did not know. I was ready for anything. I was a new person. My mom immediately noticed something had changed within me. Before I even told her the story of what had happened, she somehow knew I wasn't the old Paul. Maybe a day had passed when I sat down with her and told her the story of what God had done. With tears of joy she thanked God and, I believe, had an entirely new outlook on the power of prayer. She welcomed the "new me" with open arms. My dad, on the other hand, was (and still is) skeptical. Granted, I do not believe that he really knew to what extent alcohol controlled my life. A cradle Catholic, who has faithfully attended Holy Mass every Sunday for as long as I could remember, could not believe the healing power of Almighty God. This, as you will see, played an important role in my conversion to Catholicism, but at the time it didn't faze me because as far as I was concerned God didn't work through the Catholic Church. I was a living example of this, and my father was proving my point.

Not too long after that, I had some of my drinking friends over. Some time had passed and I noticed that being at home didn't have any effect on my desire to drink. I was still sober and I did not even think about drinking. My friends and I went for a walk around the neighborhood, and I took the opportunity to explain to them all that had happened. This news took them off guard and they really didn't know what to think. I don't blame them either, because this is the type of thing you just don't hear about every day, let alone in a group of non-religious people. They were very supportive despite not completely realizing what had taken place. After all, if I myself hadn't fully digested this, how could I expect them to? I was on fire for the Lord and wasn't afraid to show it! I was so zealous in telling them of the love and mercy that God had bestowed on me that when I look back I probably would have scared myself off! Nevertheless, they accepted the good news, despite not fully grasping its depth. Telling my own extended family what God had done would be the more difficult task. At least for me, knowing their religious standing and viewpoints, I knew it would sound far-fetched and fanatical but it nevertheless needed to be said.

My sisters and in-laws were visiting the house and this is where the moment of truth was to happen. There was no turning back after I told them. Once the entire family knew what had happened,

I knew that I would be held accountable for everything. All my actions from now on and the faithfulness with which I spoke of God's mercy and love would be put to the test. So, after I had explained the whole story to them, it would be time itself that would tell the last story. I knew that this was real. I knew that I had to be a true witness to the healing power of Jesus Christ despite all of the skepticism, and the only way to do this was through time itself. Would I continue in my new life as a new creation in Christ or would I slip and go back to the old me and give in to alcohol once more?

The news of what God had done for me is something I knew not everyone would believe. I had not known many Christians at that time, so sharing my story was somewhat difficult. After all, who would believe me if he hadn't known me or the decrepit condition which was wrought upon me by alcohol?

I now had a new home in the same church where I was healed. Each Sunday I would go back to this church and attend services. These people knew what had happened and they welcomed me. Since it was a new type of church service than what I grew up with, I had to learn (or re-learn) how things were done. I must admit, however, that I did not really get into the whole praise-and-worship aspect of the church service. For whatever reason, the music did nothing for me and I always felt uncomfortable. I nevertheless accepted this new form of worship and tried my best to embrace it. I just always felt that worship was something more reverent.

After a couple of weeks went by, our church was going to hold their annual summer picnic at the home of a member who owned a large lot of property with a pond in which a few of us were to be baptized. Although I was baptized as a baby, I was told that since I was not able, at that time, to confess my sins, then I wasn't really baptized. I hadn't come to the age of accountability yet. At the time, this made sense. After all, as they pointed out, Jesus wasn't baptized as a baby, and nowhere in Scripture did it mention baptizing babies. So I embraced this teaching and decided to get re-baptized, despite not bothering to find out why I was baptized as an infant to begin with.

I remember the day well. It was a picture-perfect day outside, I was in love with the Lord, and simply wanted to be as close to Him as possible. Therefore, I was baptized in the pond and had a new sense of being. I'm not really sure what spiritual significance that event had, but it nevertheless left me with a heart willing to be closer to our Lord.

As the weeks after my healing came and went, I found myself having to adjust to a completely different lifestyle than anything I had ever experienced. Yes, it was a new beginning and a fresh start, but at the same time this meant breaking old, familiar habits. Namely, coming to terms with emotional baggage that I carried around before and during the time I was drinking. The very reasons why, perhaps, that I began drinking in the first place. For instance, before and during my drinking days I would always be very anxious, nervous, and suffering from very low self-esteem. I literally hated waking up in the morning because it meant I had to deal with these issues again. I would try to sleep as long as possible just so I wouldn't have to face them. Sleeping was an escape from my reality. When I was drinking—I would drink until I passed out. Now that I no longer drank, I really didn't know how to fall asleep. Strange but true! I had to pray constantly for God to grant to me a new way of thinking. I would pray that I could trust Him to keep me safe from my own weaknesses. This took time, and even though I wasn't drinking I still suffered a great deal from this attitude. Reading the Scriptures and contemplating the humanness of the people involved in the stories helped me a great deal. I would place myself in their shoes and try to experience their struggles and realize that they were normal people like me, and they overcame those struggles through God's help. That aided me tremendously in my own battles with my old way of thinking. It was a blessing, as this eventually led me to an explosion of examples by way of the communion of saints, of which at this time I knew nothing.

It was only through patience and prayer that I allowed our Lord to slowly transform my way of thinking. He had to use example after example to pound into my head the trust He wanted me to have in Him. This trust was probably easier for me to embrace—more so than other people—simply because I experienced God's loving kindness in such a dramatic and real way. It left absolutely no room for doubt. Since I could not deny what God had done for me, there was no way I could deny His capabilities for me (or anyone else) in the future. I knew where I was in life and I know how hopeless my situation was at the time. God took all of that away from me. He did something in me that not even I or anyone else could ever do. He put hope into a hopeless situation in a real, tangible way. Through this I've learned that people must sincerely desire it. They must fully want to be transformed, knowing that the one Who they are being conformed to far surpasses their own expectations in life. God does work quickly in the lives of those who are eager to draw near to Him. He doesn't want to waste time.

I had to find a new church home at this time as well. Having to travel some distance to attend church service each week presented its difficulties. It wasn't practical. Therefore, I wanted to attend a church nearer to my home that held the same views I currently held. I knew that the faith I was brought up in, Lutheranism, wasn't an option any more—much to my mother's chagrin. I didn't see Christianity, as I believed it to be, in the Lutheran church, but I did in the church where I was healed. I thus concluded that Lutheranism wasn't an option because somewhere along the line, I believed, they had gone astray from the truth and from God. I based this on the fact that you just don't see such miraculous occurrences like the one I experienced in the Lutheran church. I had a very narrow mindset back then and didn't yet see the big picture. I still had a lot to learn and had come to some rash conclusions based solely on my own personal ideas and beliefs.

It was at this time that I got my first job since I so shamelessly walked away from my other job. My mom was able to get me into the same company where she had worked for the past ten years or so. This was a new horizon, and another new beginning for me. Here, I felt my faith would be put to the test and it would either be a time for me to learn or a time for me to fall. So I began working again and it was in this place of employment where I found an avenue that God used to place me where He knew I needed to be.

O my God, Your ways are mysterious.

By faith we walk with You in trust,

In full knowledge that You know what is the best for us.

My God, help me to see the path that You've

Laid out for my life, and the grace to be able to

Walk along it with boldness.

Even when we're not particularly looking or realizing it, God shapes the path we walk. Events happen for a reason and even though something might look dreary or uncertain to us, we can rest assured that since God allowed it we can trust His divine providence.

When I began my new job this was exactly the case. When we freely ask the Lord to walk before us and shape our path in life, He will do it in all areas of our life. Nothing is excluded. I didn't really know exactly what to expect at my new job. I was working with new people who never knew of my condition just months earlier. I still related to people as I did when I was drinking. After all, when drinking is part of your daily life for so long, it takes some time to break habits and thought patterns. Therefore, I still believed that people looked at me the same way as when I was drinking. I saw people picturing me as a failure in life. A bum, a nobody. But the difference this time was the fact that I knew deep down that I wasn't that person. I was a new creation. I was optimistic and had something I thought I could give to others. This gave me great hope and it allowed me to deal with these difficulties in a more positive way.

I had an authentic identity and I knew it. This new identity which now defined me, however, was foreign to most people not familiar with Christian spirituality. Christianity isn't a hobby or a system of beliefs meant to be kept in one's private life; Christianity is a way of life. It is the very source and center of our everyday lives. It decides the way we think and act. Everything in life, now, re-volved around this new truth, this new identity I had as a dignified person made in the image and likeness of God and created solely for the purpose of gaining heaven and bringing as many people as I could along with me. This was on the forefront of every endeavor I took, the goal, so-to-speak, of every encounter I had and the fruit by which I knew I was created.

I knew that God was now part of my daily life. There was no way around it; I brought Him into everything I did. No, I didn't go around preaching to everybody, nor did I sit in judgment of others, but I tried to live and work to the best of my ability and if anyone asked I would gladly tell them about my faith. This happened on a few occasions with the few people at work who knew my story and asked me to tell them about it. Other than that, it was few and far between. Nevertheless, I was glad to be on my feet again, healthy and ready to make for myself a new beginning in life!

After a few weeks on the job I began talking to a coworker of mine about the faith. Little did I realize at the time the domino effect this conversation would have in my life. He happened to be familiar with the very pastor of the church where the Lord had healed me! An instant friendship was established.

I eventually found a new church home. It was a small, storefront building at the end of a plaza converted into a church which held to the Southern Baptist tradition. An ice cream shop used to be there and so everyone called it the "Ice Cream Church." Only a handful of people made up the congregation, but God in His goodness used this church as a means to draw mostly young Hispanic kids to Christ. The attendees were made up of a diversity of many different people. Young and old, they all came together each Sunday for worship and to enjoy each other's company. Everyone was a delight to meet and they were very friendly and welcoming. I was eager to share my story with anyone who would listen. The pastor was a truly humble man of God who was willing to let me tell my story almost right away. I was delighted! It seems strange to me now, after the fact, that I was now attending a Southern Baptist church and no longer a Pentecostal church. Therefore, there were disagreements on doctrine and beliefs, but that didn't even come to my mind at the time. I figured, perhaps, that as long as they held fast to the Bible and taught what was in it, then I was okay.

In Protestant communities the Bible alone is the sole authority of faith and morals. This I realized, and at the time believed to be true. That is why I didn't even question the doctrinal differences between my former church and my new church. They taught Scripture and that alone was good enough for me. I didn't even question on whose authority their interpretation of Scripture was based. I simply had to believe the pastor was God's anointed and knew what he was talking about whenever he expounded on Scripture. It was his interpretation that mattered.

This is why we have so many differing non-Catholic churches (or, more technically, "ecclesiastical communities"); they all have their own interpretation of something that is supposed to be based on unity in belief.

Nevertheless, I continued my faith journey. I was still in love with Jesus Christ and kept to Him as best I could. Life was wonderful! I had a new job, I had a new church I could call my home, and everything was running smoothly. I had begun to attend a weekly Bible study at my new church home that was headed by my friend with whom I worked. Each Sunday was special. In my past, waking up for church was something I didn't want to do. I never understood the point. Yes, at certain times it might have meant something, but it was never something I looked forward to. Especially during my drinking days when, I remember, I actually went a few times only in mockery of it. Poking fun at the notion of being able to drink wine while at church seemed like a funny thing at the time. I am hesitant to even bring this up but I always need to remind myself of how far away from God I actually was. Church, at least at that point in my life, meant absolutely nothing to me. I remain haunted by my horrid choices. Now, I rejoiced at the fact that I was able to go to church each Sunday! It was real and it meant something.

With my new (and my first) Bible study, I was learning my faith in leaps and bounds. By God's grace the very desire I had for drinking was replaced with a desire to seek Him and know Him. Learning the faith was therefore easy for me. There had been times where I would spend hours prayerfully reading the Bible and placing myself in the very circumstances in the stories I was reading. The Bible became alive to me unlike ever before.

Scripture, I knew, was the very Word of God and I devoured it whenever I could. Everywhere I found that I could relate to the stories and learn from them how to better my own walk with Christ.

I was being taught who God is and how He operates with us and I learned how to apply it to my daily life. This was now life for me. I knew that what I read was infusing me with how God wanted me to live in order to be satisfied. It truly was as if I was thirsty and reading Scripture was the only thing satisfying me. I couldn't get enough and everything I was learning couldn't be held inside. I had to quickly tell someone about it and would exclaim with utter enthusiasm, "WOW! Did you know…?" or, "This is incredible, listen to this…!"

Along with attending church, I also got active in the community. One of the members of our church felt the call to open a housing project to help single parents get back on their feet. On several occasions I was able to help out in the restoration of the building that she was going to use—simply doing odd jobs and helping out wherever I could. On Christmas Day(s) a few of us from the church went to the local Baptist church and helped out feeding the homeless in the area. All of this volunteer work was new to me; I had never volunteered before but quickly saw how rewarding it was. While growing up, the thought of going anywhere on Christmas morning seemed out of the question. It was a day for family and celebration. Now, through volunteering, I began to realize how unfortunate a lot of people are: homeless people who have no more family left and are left alone—nothing to eat and no one to celebrate with. I was beginning to understand the meaning of selflessness. I was learning how to take the focus off of myself and begin to place focus on the needs of others. I was still able to see my family on Christmas Day, but the experience of working with the homeless truly gave me a new perspective on life.

5

A Thought...a Trail

In Your ways, O Lord, You lead us.

In faith we follow.

Show to us Your ways,

That we might become obedient.

My love for Jesus Christ was constant. Anyone knows that when we sincerely love someone we desire to know everything about him or her. Every little detail. The same is true when we sincerely love God. This is why my desire to read Sacred Scripture was something I never got tired of. That's just the nature of Sacred Scripture. It is the Living Word of God. It truly is alive; by reading and applying it to our everyday lives we find ourselves infused with the grace needed to be who God has called us to be. This is why reading Sacred Scripture never tires, it's always giving us new revelations of ourselves and of God.

After a few months, a single event occurred that would eventually change my whole perspective on Christianity—or at least cause me to see things differently. It was a phone conversation with my cousin. I cannot remember why we were discussing the topic at the time, but we were talking about the bubonic plague, or the Black Death, that swept over Europe and parts of Asia in the mid–fourteenth century, killing a major portion of the population of the time. A thought popped into my head combining three facets of life: the spiritual, temporal, and the historical. First, I recalled that in the Bible God would send plagues onto the earth to punish the wicked. Okay, simple enough. Second, the thought of whether or not God still does this in our day, or at least up to the time of the fourteenth century. And third—probably the most important aspect of what came to my mind that day—was why we, as Christians, looked to the end of the book of the Acts of the Apostles as the end of what we could define as events authentically coming from God himself. In other words, when we read what happened in Sacred Scripture—the plagues, the events of people's lives, etc., and especially in the book of Acts—we can safely say that these events were truly actions of God. The thought occurred to me that we could not define any event in world history as being an authentic act of God if it were not written in the Bible—which we know to be the true Word of God, without error. All of these questions were unrolled for me in time and through God's grace and they will be explained throughout this book. Everything is mystically interconnected; to answer these questions at mere face value would be doing an injustice to divine revelation.

The book of the Acts is an historical book as much as it is a divinely inspired book. Consequently, as these three thoughts came to mind I had to do some research. Some of the questions I had to ask myself were, "Why can't we say with absolute certainty that certain world events that took place after the Acts of the Apostles was written were in fact punishments from God on humanity?" I also asked myself, "God has not stopped working in the lives of Christians since the book of Acts ended, so would it be plausible to say that the book of Acts could technically still be taking place?" To me it seems obvious, since the central theme of the book of Acts does not have an ending, and events continue to unfold in our time. Even unto our day today! So, I asked myself, "How is it that we can trust the words in the book of Acts as being authentically being the actual events of the Holy Spirit and of the entire Trinity, but cannot say with absolute certainty that events that took place after the book of Acts weren't the work of the Holy Spirit?"

The debate wasn't necessarily about whether or not the Black Death was a punishment from God, but whether the Bible was the sole means by which God's truth is captured. After all, since God hasn't stopped working in the lives of believers since the book of Acts was written, why then could we not say that there was more to Christianity than simply the Bible? In others words, were we still, today, living out the book of Acts? This isn't, by any means, to say that the canon of Sacred Scripture is not complete. Rather, the works which we see the Holy Spirit doing in Sacred Scripture, especially in the book of Acts, He is still doing to this very day.

This notion only served to increase my studies. Previously, my interest of study was by means of the Bible alone. Don't get me wrong; the Bible is the best research for studying the things of God, but now my interest was drawn to a more historical aspect of our faith. Boosted by this thought of history and Christianity, I wanted to learn how Christianity was lived not simply in my own generation or my parents' and grandparents' generations, but how it was lived for hundreds of years before. Therefore, my thought of whether or not the bubonic plague was of God or not brought me to look up the Christianity of that particular time period, which was the 1300s.

A friend and I visited the local community college in order to check their library to see if we could find any books on the subject. At this time, I don't believe that my friend knew of my initial motive in researching books on Christian history. I figured that since I grew up in a Lutheran church I might as well look up books written by its founder, Martin Luther. I didn't know at the time that Luther came some 300 years after the Black Death occurred, but it was a starting point. Plus, I was somewhat curious of his own commentary on Scripture as compared to how we see Scripture today. Luckily, the library had quite a few books either written by or about Luther. I was delighted, but the funny thing is that the very first thing I read out of a book on Luther (the book was basically a dictionary on Luther's beliefs) was that he saw the pope as being the antichrist! Yes, back in the 16th century they were already trying to determine who was the antichrist! This is still so prevalent today in many Christian communities. At any rate, I sat down and read from a few of the books. Since I didn't have a library card, I wasn't able to check out any of the books, but I was determined to continue my studies elsewhere.

I didn't own a computer at the time, so trying to find reading material was rather difficult. Nevertheless, I was able to find some books at the local Christian bookstores. I bought book after book written by Martin Luther and other Reformers, and books about Christian history in general. I was consuming all the reading material that I could. This was food for my soul because it shed light on not only what Scripture taught through commentary, but being an avid "student" of history allowed me to learn how Christians lived hundreds of years ago!

As I look back at my journey during this time, I wonder why I had never thought to look into Christianity's first 1500 years or so. In the many books I bought about Christian history, the narratives seemed to jump from the book of Acts to the time of the Protestant Reformation, with very little about the time in between. It didn't occur to me—at least not at that time.

I recall reading about the Christians who were persecuted by the Catholic Church because they had disagreed with it; men such as John Hus, John Wycliffe, and William Tyndale. I wondered why they were so harshly treated if they were only trying to proclaim what they saw to be the truth. Granted, I hadn't done a thorough study on the lives of these men, but from what I read I was appalled. This only added fuel, so to speak, to my conviction that the Catholic Church was a "man-made" Christian religion. But despite all of this, I still saw beauty within Christian history even during the time of these persecutions. At the time I believed that the Church consisted of men and women who believed Jesus Christ was their personal Lord and Savior, no matter what "denomination" they were in. Little did I know early in my studies exactly how Christian denominations formed. I thought that as long as one adhered to Sacred Scripture as the sole authority and sole rule of faith, one was a follower of Jesus Christ. Certain things hadn't yet occurred to me. Things such as how we can know for certain that what these men taught is exactly how God intended Scripture to be interpreted, or who has the final say as to whose interpretation of Scripture is correct and whose is false. I guess, at this point, true doctrine and that ever-so-feared word "dogma" really meant nothing to me. I saw doctrine and dogma as a hindrance to true Christianity, but it never dawned on me that it was necessary in order to rightfully understand what God communicated to His people.

What it boiled down to was authority. What Church had the authority to claim that their interpretation of Sacred Scripture was the interpretation God intended? How would I know with absolute certainty that what I was hearing in the sermons at my Southern Baptist church was really the interpretation God desired? Scriptural interpretation was heavy on my mind. How would I know that what the Southern Baptists taught was authentic, as opposed to what my former Pentecostal church was teaching? They had agreed on many things but it would be foolish to deny that they were in agreement on everything. This held true for the other Protestant churches including the church I was baptized in (the first time), the Lutheran church. So the question remained: Whose interpretation of Scripture is authentic? Keep in mind that I am not implying that all denominations teach complete falsehoods. No, rather, certain key elements of Christianity differed and I wanted to know why. I was restless to find out what was missing. How could all these denominations exist and all claim to be following the same Jesus? Didn't Jesus preach unity within His Church? Where was this unity in heart and mind?

All of this study and all of this research never lessened. I still had a zeal and a fire for the things of God and I wanted to know more and more about Him. In light of my experience I simply wanted to know intimately the very One who loved me so much that He granted me a second chance at life. I didn't fear where He was taking me. I knew He was up to something, but at the time I had no idea what it was.

6

Catholicism 101: A Crash Course in Theology

O my Jesus,

You are Truth.

Let not my feet slip into error.

I was at work one afternoon and had some time to kill after my shift, so I decided to walk down to the bookstore in the mall to see if they had any books of interest. As I panned over the religion section of the bookstore, a book called *The Lost Books of the Bible and the Forgotten Books of Eden* jumped out at me. This piqued my interest, so I began to look through it, wondering what types of books they might be referring to. To my wonderment, it had the books of Christ's infancy, a book about Mary the Mother of God and her own infancy, different books about the Apostles, and much more. This was something I knew I had to look into. After all, why weren't these books included in Scripture? I didn't know but I wanted to find out. So I bought the book and began to read it.

At the time, I had never put any thought into how we got the books of the Bible. Who chose which ones to keep and which ones not to keep? At what point in time did this happen? After all, the Apostles had the Old Testament but no New Testament when they lived and preached the Word of God. I realized that somewhere along the line the books of the New Testament had to have been added somehow by someone. Who had the authority to claim that the books we now read in the New Testament are truly infallible? After all, the books themselves never mention which books are infallible. It had to be a source somewhere outside Scripture that made such a decision. Furthermore, why weren't the books I was reading about in this bookstore not considered infallible, and who made that decision? I wasn't inquiring as to *"if"* the books we read in the New Testament are infallible, but *who* made the decision that they were, and what criteria they used in coming to that conclusion.

These kinds of thoughts plagued me. They were logical inquiries, and I wanted to know. In no way was I questioning the authority of Scripture, but I simply wanted to know how the books we now read in the New Testament came about. It puzzled me that I was never taught this in catechism class growing up. To me it was as much a part of my Christian faith and heritage as going to church each Sunday and knowing what we believe and profess.

This forced me to have to look into Catholicism for the very first time. My view of the Catholic Church was one of a sheep gone astray. At that time I believed that the Catholic Church, at one point in history, probably taught authentic Christianity. But somewhere along the line they veered off the narrow path and began teaching man-made doctrines. After all, Catholics whom I knew didn't know anything about the Bible or Christianity in general! To me, Catholicism was dead and people were merely being fooled.

So in my attempt to understand and find out how we got the books of the Bible, I was forced to look into history—which forced me to look into Catholicism. In knew that the Reformers of the Protestant tradition I grew up with and the denomination I was attending now didn't choose which books were to go into the New Testament. I knew Jesus didn't tell us and neither did His Apostles in what they wrote in the New Testament manuscripts. I was forced to look outside the Bible for the answers. This went hand-in-hand with my previous question as to the continuation of the Acts of the Apostles. Things were beginning to come together and make sense.

As I was thumbing through my new book's table of contents, one particular author's name stuck out: Polycarp. I had never heard the name before and was interested as to what this Polycarp had to say. I saw that he had written a letter to the church in Philippi, just as the Apostle Paul had. What kind of letter/book was this? It read almost verbatim with the letters in the New Testament; I was intrigued. It truly sounded as if it could have been one of the New Testament books. It read the same as a New Testament letter, and it taught us the same truths that the New Testament has. In fact, this Polycarp references the Apostle Paul in his letter. Plus, the story of the martyrdom of Polycarp was included.

His letter wasn't like the rest of the books in this "Forgotten Books of the Bible" book. It read not as a book with just an interesting story based on events left out of Scripture. It read with conviction. Not in the same conviction that we see in the New Testament letters, but a conviction that confirmed what we read in the New Testament. It was almost as if it were a continuation of it. Come to find out, this Polycarp was a real person! He was a student of the Apostle John, the disciple whom Jesus loved. I was absolutely astounded by this. Here was the beginning of an answer to my question about the continuation of the book of

Acts. Polycarp was only one of many Apostolic Fathers who took the baton from the Apostles and ran with it—the next generation of Christians after the Apostles had died.

I was never taught about the Apostolic Fathers. Why? They play a vital role in understanding Christianity today. This was the link that connects Scripture and history. The very thing I was looking for! Where was this headed? It was a whole new realm to me, yet at the same time the vast majority of my fellow Christians could not see the importance of this. Since it wasn't in the Bible I was told that I should take these writings with a grain of salt. In other words, what they had to say may be worthwhile and good, but we cannot know for certain that everything they say is true. I saw it differently. Of course I understood it wasn't written in the same nature that Sacred Scripture was. But I looked at it as authentic Christianity during the second generation since Christ's ascension. This was how Christians lived after the time of the Apostles.

It wasn't so much the contents of Polycarp's writings I was focusing on (which aligned with Sacred Scripture anyway) but the reality that Christianity continued in truth and practice after the events of the book of Acts. They had the teachings of the Apostles, who received their teachings from Christ Himself. I understood that at this point in history the books of the New Testament were just completed and the Christians of the time hadn't yet decided which writings were infallible. They had no New Testament, but Christianity was nevertheless thriving. They had no New Testament to base their beliefs on, yet how was it, I asked myself, that what they practiced could be considered authentic Christianity according to today's Christian (Protestant) understanding?

Another question that dawned on me at this time revolved around the timing for when the books of the New Testament were compiled. When and by whom? After all, wouldn't it make sense that whoever had the authority to discern which of the many books/letters written in the first century of Christianity were inspired by the Holy Spirit and by God Himself, had *also* been given this authority by God through Jesus Christ? And wouldn't it make sense that whoever had this God-given authority should be the one I listen to for real, authentic answers to questions I had? If I couldn't trust the authority that told me which books were inspired and which books weren't, then wouldn't it make sense that I wouldn't be able to even trust the New Testament to begin with as being truly inspired?

At about this same time, and from reading the story of the heroic martyrdom of Polycarp, I was drawn specifically to the martyrs—those faithful men and women of the early Church who suffered terribly for the name of Jesus Christ and died, oftentimes very violent deaths, for His Name's sake. Finding *Foxe's Book of Martyrs* was instrumental in the development of my love for the martyrs. I read story after story of men and women who were just like us and had what it took to endure the most horrific treatment and remain faithful. I was so utterly inspired by their example that I longed to see what it was inside of them that made them so courageous. What was it that sustained them throughout their countless tortures? I wanted it too! I saw the love they had for Jesus, the ultimate love anyone can give, and desired to possess it myself. Who were these people and why was I never taught about them?

Come to find out, the Early Church was flooded with martyrs of all ranks and ages! All of these faithful men and women belonged to a Church that didn't have a New Testament, but they understood exactly what they were dying for. I didn't see this type of heroic Christianity within the faith traditions I was a part of in my previous experiences. I had read stories of the few Christian martyrs of the Middle Ages who were unjustly martyred by the Catholics, but I was seeing something different here. It wasn't a supposed Christian murdering another supposed Christian, but pagans murdering Christians. This was something altogether wholesome and there was something substantially unifying about the entire episode.

I had noticed a common theme about the Apostolic Fathers that, at the time, I had to skim over because I felt it no longer applied to Christianity today. It was the fact that a lot of what they wrote sounded "Catholic." All the talk of bishops and Rome and the Eucharist didn't pertain to me or the Christianity I was used to, so I basically paid no close attention to it. After all, I thought, Catholicism was dead. It was a religion of man-made rules that no longer pertain to authentic Christianity. This was difficult, however, because although it took a while for it to dawn on me, I thought to myself: How could these faithful men and women who had the faith and courage to give up their very lives for Jesus be Catholic if Catholicism was such a false version of Christianity? Why would anyone willingly surrender himself to violent torture for something that wasn't true? One might think that perhaps the Catholicism we see in the time of the generation after the Apostles differed from the Catholicism we see today. I later found out that this is not true at all! Far from it! But at the time thoughts such as these didn't occur to me. I simply wanted to be able to imitate and learn from the example of these men and women in order to better serve Jesus Christ myself. The actual doctrine concerned me little. Granted, I embraced what didn't sound Catholic and denied what did sound Catholic.

By sheer ignorance I was picking and choosing what I wanted to believe to be true, and disregarding the rest without even allowing the teachings that I disagreed with a chance to explain themselves. For instance, it had never occurred to me to ask myself why these early Christians venerated Mary, or believed that Jesus Christ was truly present in the Eucharist, or believed some of the doctrines that I, personally, did not believe.

A little while later, and after researching the Apostolic Fathers, I discover what was called the Early Church Fathers. These men also acted as a continuation of the book of Acts. I learned that in generation after generation after the passing of the Apostles, other Christians who adhered to and taught exactly what the Apostle taught (without a canonized New Testament) wrote letters, treatises, books, testimonies, and even some poems! I was fully immersed in what I was longing for! Christianity lived from one generation to another, all of which was documented. The thread of historical Christianity that I was seeking to learn was unveiling itself before me. I began to see something that would change my understanding of the Christian religion forever.

I didn't have a computer at the time, and had some difficulty trying to find the writings of the Apostolic Fathers and the Early Church Fathers. Libraries around the area might have a volume here and a volume there. I soon found out that the complete set of the writings from the Apostolic Fathers through the last Early Church Father was a 38-volume set! Since there was no way I could afford this set, I was discouraged because I couldn't continue my studies. As God would have it, He saw the desire in my heart and acted on it! A coworker of mine had mentioned to me that if he received a new job he would sell me his computer and buy a new one for himself. Well, not too long after having told me this, he did find a job! Surely the writings of the Fathers could be found online!

Now that I had the Internet at my disposal, I was ready to do some serious digging. I quickly found websites that had the entire 38 volumes of the writings of the Early Church Fathers. Since I couldn't get comfortable reading books in front of a computer screen, I thought of a brilliant idea. I went to the local dollar store and bought several three-ring binders, then went to the local office supply shop and stocked up on paper and a hole punch. I sat there in front of my computer for hours on end, printing out volume after volume of the Church Fathers, punching holes in the paper, and placing them into the three-ring binders. I went so far as to even create a catchy cover piece and glue it onto the binder so I knew who and what it was! To this day, I still have roughly 20-30 binders full of the writings of the Church Fathers!

Day after day I would study. I was captivated by the lives of the early Christians. I would read sermons, treatises, letters, and books—one after another, trying to piece together what exactly it was that the first Christians believed, taught, and how they lived. Just being able to read the stories inked by the very heroic people whose lives were surrendered to Jesus Christ, even to the point of martyrdom, inspired me to such an extent that on several occasions, after I had read an incredible account, I felt so full of zeal that I had to tell my fellow Christians about it as soon as possible! On quite a few occasions I would bring some of the writings I had recently read; a few of us would gather and I would literally read the accounts aloud to them.

It's interesting to note that all of the "Catholic" terminology that the Church Fathers used was simply ignored by us at the time; we were skimming over those items but soaking in the rest of the wise advice they had to offer. I saw Christianity as being something that ran across the board. It didn't matter what specific denomination people belonged to, as long as they adhered to the Bible and believed Jesus was their Lord and Savior. Whether one was a Catholic, Lutheran, Pentecostal, Baptist, or from another group wasn't important.

However, certain questions kept arising in my mind. For instance, since Christianity looked so different today than it did when the Church Fathers lived, what had gone wrong? Why weren't we worshiping like they worshiped? Why don't Christians today behave the way they behaved back then? Was "our" version of Christianity wrong, since it didn't mirror the Christianity we see in the earliest years of the faith? I always thought Christianity was the same ever since the time of the Apostles. At least I believed that it was supposed to be.

The bottom line was that something didn't line up. Something was missing, and I felt that somehow Christians today are doing the Christianity of the first several hundred years a grave injustice. But what was it? How did we end up looking, acting, behaving, and believing what we do today? Only a close study of the history of our faith could answer this question. I knew that I couldn't rely on only one era of church history to find my answer but would have to learn more about Christianity throughout its entire existence! This was an undertaking that I knew would take some time and patience. Two thousand years is certainly a hefty load for anyone to bear! Plus, where could I find my information from a non-biased point of view? After all, at this point I was giving the Catholic perspective more credit than I would have just a few months prior, because of the witness of the Church Fathers and the martyrs. But I wasn't satisfied with the differences. I needed to know how the Christianity we see today got to be the way it is.

At about this time another factor came into play. I recall channel surfing one day and I came upon a Catholic television network. They were showing some form of worship that I had never seen before. It took place in a huge but empty church building that looked completely covered in gold. It was breathtaking! But what were they doing? Several priests slowly walked in, singing some ancient chant that had such a mystical reverence to it. It wasn't sung in English so I had no idea what it was they were saying, but whatever it was, I was completely captivated by it. The priests then reached the altar and knelt down in front of what looked like a golden sunburst that was sitting on top of the altar. What in the world was that? I was utterly drawn to it; something inside of me was in awe and reverence. Then the priests began to say a prayer (in English) that I had never heard, and still to this day is my favorite prayer. They began invoking the name of Jesus in His Sacred Heart. What was His Sacred Heart? Obviously Jesus has a heart, but what was this prayer all about? I never heard anyone pray to Jesus' heart before. As I listened, the most beautiful words I ever heard were being prayed by these priests:

*Heart of Jesus; Son of the Eternal Father;
have mercy on us.*

*Heart of Jesus; formed in the womb of the
Virgin Mary by the Holy Ghost;
have mercy on us.*

*Heart of Jesus; full of goodness and love;
have mercy on us.*

*Heart of Jesus; most worthy of all praise;
have mercy on us...*

And it continued. The invocation of mercy from the very heart of Jesus Himself! I thought this was so profound and so intimate that I couldn't see anything more loving coming from the mouth of any Christian! To make it more meaningful to me, at this point, was the fact that everything these priests prayed was absolutely Scriptural! And these were Catholics! Things began making more and more sense to me. I began to piece things together, from what I was reading from the Early Church Fathers and the martyrs and their heroic example of being witnesses to Christ and now this, modern-day Catholicism! Parallels were being drawn and the pieces of God's divine puzzle were being put together with great intensity. A marvelous picture was beginning to develop.

At first I was hesitant to tell anyone about what I saw and especially how I felt about it. I could clearly foresee what their reaction would be. After all, I was even somewhat frightened at the idea of having truly felt the presence of God in what seemed like a superstitious ritual. Nevertheless, I could not deny it. How could someone who was supposedly superstitious speak or pray to God in such a beautiful way? It didn't make sense. What was that sunburst-looking thing they were kneeling in front of? I wanted to know. It was mystifying and it completely drew me to it; I couldn't keep my eyes off of it. Even more, I admired how reverent the priests were. They were decked in fancy robes and their actions were humble and not proud. In a sense it felt as if that was how our soul was to act before God—in complete Godly fear and humility. I always looked at the Catholic Church with its pomp and ceremony as being un-Christian. Why all the gold and fancy robes? Why make the Church look so beautiful and not humble, as Christ was? After having this experience, I saw the Catholic Church in a new light, but I still had a lot of questions.

I began watching this Catholic television network more and more. They televised daily Mass several times throughout the day and I watched it as often as I could. I had never been to a Catholic Mass before, except for the time I went with my catechism class in the Lutheran church simply to see how other Christians worshiped God. But of course back then I couldn't have cared less, because I didn't know Christ. This time I knew Him and I saw the Catholic Mass as strange, but I longed to find out why they did what they did. I continued to think of how the Early Christians lived and what they taught with all of their Catholic views, and configured it to what I was watching on TV. What made me even more interested is that at times during the Mass the priest mentioned the names of some of the martyrs whose lives have touched mine and inspired me to be more bold in my own walk with Christ. I thought to myself, "These guys profess to be acquainted with the martyrs of the early church!" What was the connection, I wondered? Catholicism, in my estimate, had gone astray long ago, but the martyrs never did. It wasn't until a while later that I realized that what the martyrs and the Church Fathers taught was the very same thing that these Catholic priests were talking about and preaching!

Another aspect of the Catholic Mass that drew me in was the use of the Latin language. To me, it was so reverent and respectful, two characteristics I found lacking in most Protestant services. But why were they praying some parts of the Mass in Latin and not in English? I was not familiar with Latin, but there was something special about praying to Jesus in that ancient language. I wanted to learn more. I wanted questions answered, so I prayed earnestly for God to grant me the knowledge to understand.

In my attempt to unravel the questions that filled my mind, I always remained centered on the love of Jesus Christ. It was Him who placed these questions within me. I desired to know Christianity from start to finish. As a result, I began buying book after book written about the history of Christianity. What I noticed, however, is that there really wasn't an unbiased view. Some were written by non-Catholic Christians who recognized the Catholicity of the early church but quickly skimmed over the 1500 years before the Protestant Reformation in the 16th century. The other books written with a Catholic perspective didn't seem to do the Reformation justice. I knew for a fact that the hand of God moves both within the Catholic Church and outside the Catholic Church. What I didn't understand was why there wasn't unity all throughout Christianity's history. Each seemed to follow one theme or another, depending on who wrote the book. Certainly Jesus didn't intend for this to happen.

One of the best books on Christian history that I read during this time was written by an Early Church Father named Eusebius. Eusebius lived during the lifetime of the first Christian emperor of Rome, named Constantine, around the year 325 A.D. He gave a detailed description of what Christianity looked like from the time of the Apostles until his day in the early fourth century. He mainly used quotes from other Church Fathers, to clearly show the faith in which he had been taught. Now, what made Eusebius' work stand out above the rest of the books I read on Church history was that he used actual quotes from those who received the faith straight from the Apostles themselves in oral form. I learned a few key components in how to understand which Church was the true Church that Jesus established.

7

Hard Doctrines and Divine Grace

Jesus, I trust in You.

One point that kept coming back to me was the fact that the Christian faith had to rely on the oral accounts given by the Apostles to their students and then to the next generations to come. The New Testament had been written by the time of Constantine but it hadn't been canonized. It wasn't yet declared the inspired infallible Word of God until several years later. With this in mind, I recognized the importance of authority, the authority which Catholics believed to rest in the pope. Non-Catholic Christians reject the notion of papal authority, of course, and as a result their own take on how the canon of the New Testament came about differs, depending on who's telling the story. After all, if they were to recognize the Catholic Church's authority in terms of defining Biblical authenticity, they would be forced to recognize the Catholic Church's other claims as well. Reason tells us that if non-Catholics accept the Catholic Church's God-given authority to declare Sacred Scripture infallible, and yet reject the Catholic Church's authority when declaring other Catholic dogmas infallible, then how can they rightfully trust the New Testament books to be authentically infallible? This would go against their teaching of Sola Scriptura, or Sacred Scripture as the sole rule and authority of their faith. Therefore, non-Catholic authors on Christian history had to reason their way around Christian history in order to fit their own faith tradition.

It was beginning to make sense to me now. There was a missing link somewhere, and authority was key. Throughout my life I never knew what the role of the pope was. In all honesty, since the Catholic Church calls the pope the Vicar of Christ, and without ever being told what that means, I assumed that Catholics believed the pope was Christ on earth. I even thought that perhaps Catholics worshiped the pope. I didn't know. But now God was beginning to unravel this deep mystery to me. I always thought that Scripture was to be interpreted by the reader, who was inspired by the Holy Spirit. Scripture certainly is inspired by Him, but it has to be viewed in light of everything else in Scripture. Far too many people take a single verse from Bible and run with it. They blindly disregard other chapters and verses that might conflict with that verse. As a result, we see so many interpretations of the same passages. Subsequently, different faith traditions develop, and before you realize it, confusion sets in and we no longer have a grasp on truth itself. I understood that when Jesus had given the keys of the kingdom to Peter, He gave him the infallible authority, through the Holy Spirit, to safeguard the teachings from error. Peter, and his successors, the popes, stood as the final say in what was in line with what Christ Himself taught and what wasn't. He could not add anything nor could he subtract anything. He could only guard it from being twisted, misused. He could infallibly declare something in error or heretical. This was not on his own authority, but by the power of the Holy Spirit given to him by Jesus Himself. This made complete sense. When you take a look around today we see so many different faith traditions all claiming to be the inspired Word of God in truth. However, since the majority of them contradict or disagree with one another on different matters which Jesus taught, chaos results and the faithful are led astray and cannot tell with absolute certainty what is the truth of what Jesus taught. Yes, they will have aspects of the whole, but not the fullness thereof.

Without turning this into an exhaustive treatise on papal authority, I'll leave it at this. I understood why there was a pope and why Jesus instituted the papacy, with all of the bishops in succession from the Apostles. Once I was completely convinced of the importance of the pope and why we need him, I felt led to read some of the writings of the popes. Thank God for technology, because at no other time in history would this be possible except for now! I found just about every encyclical, letter, apostolic constitution, homily, etc. that the popes have written throughout the ages. From the First Letter of St. Peter in Sacred Scripture to the writings of Pope Benedict XVI. I was absolutely floored at what the popes wrote. These are true Christians. Faithful and in love with Jesus Christ! I thought, how could any Christian miss these writings of such deep meaning and usefulness?

I read the writings of the popes in a new light, now that I understood their role. They truly are shepherds! They didn't ask to be deified. In my studies on the papacy, I'll be the first to admit that there were periods throughout the Church's history where the actions of certain popes were deplorable. For example, Pope Stephen VI in the ninth century had his predecessor Pope Formosus' body exhumed, put on trial, de-fingered, and thrown into the Rhine River! Pope John XII had a mistress, murdered several people, and was shot by a man whose wife he was sleeping with! Or who can forget about Pope Urban VI, who complained that he did not hear enough screaming from the cardinals when they were being tortured for conspiring against him! Even despite these horrific periods of Church history, I understood that the authority of the pope did not rest on the man, but on what he had been given. Yes, their behavior was absolutely sinful and wicked, but their behavior does not speak for the Church Herself; these men in no way altered the official teachings of the Church to sanction their sinful actions. I've also heard arguments about the Catholic Church being invalid because of the Crusades and the Inquisition. However a close study of each event reveals something far less dramatic than popular belief would have you think. But once again, these events speak not on behalf of the Church or Her teachings.

The Lord had shown to me the primacy of the chair of St. Peter, the pope, in a way that had never been explained to me before. I embraced this new revelation. It brought me comfort to know that Jesus Himself saw fit to give to us a protector of the truth which He taught. Not someone to add to it or subtract from it, but to keep it safe from error. Another piece of the divine puzzle was being connected.

Even with all of the awe I experienced as I learned about the authority of the Church built upon Peter, I still had many questions about Catholicism and was in no way ready or comfortable with becoming one. The papacy made sense, but what about the whole Mary thing? Surely the Catholic Church took the role of Mary too far. Perhaps it was this that caused the downfall of Catholicism, I thought. Even while understanding the role of the Church Fathers and the authority of the pope, I still didn't see Catholics as Christians, because all the Catholics I knew were not showing any enthusiasm or fire for Christ. What was the problem? What was missing? When and how did all these Catholics of today fall away from what the Catholics from of old declared with their own blood?

The Lord then directed my attention to His Mother, Mary. At this point I believed that she was simply the vessel that God the Father used to bring His Son into the world, as most Protestant Christians confirm. However, since the Catholic Church holds

Mary in such high esteem, I felt drawn to study why this is so. After all, I was so elated when discovering the truth about the papacy; I thought that maybe the truth the Catholics believed about Mary might be another such delight. I went into my studies open minded and was ready for nothing short of blasphemy.

It started with simple prayer. After all, I didn't know, at this time, if what I was asking of God was indeed blasphemous or legit. I made this clear to Him. Before long I was drawn toward the Holy Rosary. I've heard priests describe the prayer of the Holy Rosary as the prayer of the Gospel, so it seemed enough for me, having loved the Gospels, to at least look into this claim. So I began to do research on how the Rosary was prayed and all that was entailed in it. All I knew at this point was that it invoked Mary (who is not God) through prayer, and since I didn't understand the communion of saints teaching, this was treading on thin ice. I saw prayer as a form of worship, and since the Rosary was praying to Mary I believed that this was worshiping her.

So I began to look online at the actual words prayed in the Holy Rosary. Since it was called the prayer of the Gospel, I thought, "Well, at least I'll try to hold Catholics to their word." Little did I realize, upon researching this prayer, that it included a deep reflection on certain vital events in the life of Jesus. What was more is that the actual "Hail Mary" prayer is straight from the Gospels! "Hail Mary, full of grace, the Lord is with you" was spoken by the angel Gabriel to Mary in Luke 1:28. The phrase, "Blessed are you among woman and blessed is the fruit of your womb" was exclaimed in Luke 1:42 by Elizabeth, Mary's cousin, when Mary visited her after being told she was to bear a son. "Holy Mary, Mother of God" is mentioned in Luke 1:43, when Elizabeth announces Mary's arrival. "Pray for us sinners now, and at the hour of our death" only serves as a fulfillment of what the Apostle Paul tells us to do in 1 Timothy 2:1, that supplications, prayers, intercessions, and thanksgivings be made for all men. Since, therefore, it made sense to me that physical death does not separate believers in the Living Body of Christ, it seemed reasonable to ask the souls already in heaven to pray to God for us (as we do in the Holy Rosary), and that thought was actually very comforting.

Not only was the Hail Mary prayer Scriptural, but the main focus of the Rosary itself, the meditations on the various aspects of Jesus' life, was practically as if one was reading the very Gospels themselves! Why would anyone, I thought, desire not to pray the Holy Rosary?

I did not know this and was shocked to find this out! Almost immediately, I began to see the value in this prayer. But at the same time, I wondered why it was centered around Mary. Yes, it was quoting the Gospels, but what role did she have to play? Why did Catholics have to include such a focus on her in this prayer straight from Sacred Scripture? The prayer itself was lovely and I could clearly see how it could help someone grow in his spiritual communion with God, by way of quoting Scripture and getting familiar with the events of Christ's life, but what did Mary have to do with it?

When I first felt compelled to actually pray the Rosary, I felt very uneasy. I had the horrible thought that I might perhaps be committing a sacrilege for speaking (or in this case praying) to Mary instead of God. However, after placing my complete trust in the Providence of God and realizing that God knows the true intent of my heart, I began to pray the Rosary with more fervor, knowing that there was more to this than I realized. I had to trust Him. Otherwise, from my belief concerning Mary, what I was do-ing was drawing me away from God instead of toward Him.

Little by little, again, things began to make sense to me. I was reading about all of the Marian apparitions that had taken place throughout time and took careful notice at the number of miracles that happened during and after these visitations. It was undeniable. I learned that in order for a miracle to be truly authentic it had to go through a rigorous investigation by the Church. Out of thousands of reported miracles that had taken place, only a handful have been deemed authentic by the Church. However, this isn't to say all of the other miracles are not authentic, but they simply have never undergone the Church's investigation process. Since the Lord had performed a miracle in me, I was very fond of these things.

One particular night, after studying all things Mary, I prayed to the Lord something like this:

> *"Father, I cannot deny what You have done in my life. Nor can I deny the miracles that happened to your people during and after Mary's (supposed) appearance. Please, Lord, open my heart and my mind to the truth about Mary and her role in my life."*

Not long after this, I was reading Dr. Scott Hahn's book *Hail, Holy Queen* outside on a clear, crisp, summer afternoon. I was absolutely floored at all of the Biblical references to Mary, which I had never seen before, especially all of the Old Testament types and prefigurements of Mary. I had never been taught about these! And rightfully so; coming from a Protestant background, we didn't think twice about Mariology. Yet here it stood, even in the early Church, and in front of my face the whole time. I recall a light bulb going off inside of me, and I turned my gaze towards the sky and said aloud, "My God! It's true, ALL of it!" I understood that we do not pray to Mary as we pray in worship to God, but pray to her in terms of asking her to pray to God for and with us! She is not God and never will be. She doesn't take the place of Him but points us to Him. I concretely knew that the role that Mary plays was and is bigger than I ever imagined!

My heart was open to receive all that God would teach me

about her. The Holy Rosary came alive and it stood firm as a vital tool to grow closer to God now that I knew Mary's role. I will not go into great detail about the specific Church teachings on Mary and her role in the Christian life; I'll leave that to the experts. But for now suffice it to say that in an extraordinary way God placed within my heart an understanding, a revelation of sorts, of Mary and how her role is vital in God's salvation history, not only in Biblical times as God-bearer but in our time today as well.

But it goes deeper than this. Jumping ahead in my story, I can relate a few instances in which Mary revealed her love for me and her motherly affection. Once I was struggling with a cross that our Lord asked me to bear, and I was really downcast and almost depressed about the whole thing. It was one of those instances where our adversary the devil and his fiends play mind games with us and are so convincing in their lies that we are often struck dumb. I had a dream that I was inside of a Church. I was standing in the aisle in the back of the church and Mary, covered in light and appearing almost transparent, was about ten or fifteen rows in front of me standing among a bunch of little children. These children were all laughing, playing, and hugging Mary, while I just watched all of this play out. I then approached her myself, once all the children left, and just stood next to her. She was looking intently at the altar the whole time. After what seemed like only a few seconds, she turned her head and looked at me! She smiled and put her arm around my shoulders. At this, I fell to my knees and just wept. I was immediately infused with confidence and love. I knew instantly that what I was struggling with was taken care of and that I had nothing to fear. I woke up that morning a new person! I was revived and truly understood the motherly role of Mary in my life!

Another instance where Our Lady revealed her maternal love to me was when I had a stomach virus. For the entire day I was miserable. I couldn't keep anything down, I had a very difficult time trying to sleep, and I was dehydrated and downright out for the count. That evening as I went to bed I knew I had to work early in the morning and didn't want to call in sick. After working at the same job for several years now, I had never called in sick, so it was something I wasn't used to. I woke up in the middle of the night, about three hours or so before I had to get up. I was still suffering the effects of this virus at the time, and saw that there was nothing I could do to rid myself of this sad state of affairs. Then it dawned on me, and I prayed:

> "Mary, if everything the Catholic Church tells me about you is indeed true, please ask your Son if He could relieve my suffering so I might be able to work."

I ended up falling right back to sleep. I woke up with my alarm clock and it actually took me a few minutes to realize that my symptoms had disappeared! I was revived and had energy! I literally felt great, as if I never had a sickness to begin with. This was another way in which our Lord showed to me that His Mother is always there to help us. God had revealed to me even more supernatural instances where if it hadn't been for the intercession of His Mother they wouldn't have happened.

There have been a few other occasions where I have come to know Our Lady on a more personal level. I will not relate all of them here, but I will say that they have led me closer to Jesus Christ. I truly understand the meaning behind Christ's words on the cross, when He said to His Mother, "Woman, behold your son; son, behold your Mother."

Mary has such a beautiful way of drawing us toward her Son. As a non-Catholic I was not able to understand this. But after Our Lady had revealed to me the person of whom exactly she is, I was left in a spirit of utter wonderment. How beautiful, I thought. This is wonderful that God the Father gave her to us.

How and why non-Catholic Christians refuse her aid, help, and prayers is something I can relate to, based on my previous beliefs, but now seems incongruous with the historical Christian belief in the communion of saints.

However, as with many other Catholic teachings, the role of Mary has been abused and needs to be addressed. Places—especially in Middle America—where "Mary worship" seems to be evident have created concern in the ears of many Protestants. What, they may ask, do Catholics make of this, the ever-present excess of Mary and the watering down of Jesus? The Church specifically states that Mary is not to take the place of Christ, nor is she supposed to even be on par with Him. The Catechism of the Catholic Church states that Mary "is acknowledged and honored as being truly the Mother of God and of the redeemer" (CCC #963, quoting from *Lumen Gentium*). That is it. She is acknowledged and honored. Whether or not people do more homage than what is appropriate, only God knows. The fact remains that Mary is not to be worshiped, nor can she take the place of Jesus Christ her Son, although she is exalted above every other created being, but she still pales in comparison to Her Son, Jesus.

God, in His loving kindness, reveals things to us not only intellectually but also spiritually, in our hearts, for more clarity and conviction. It's one thing to "know" something and it's another thing to make it a reality in one's everyday life. We can "know" Jesus by understanding who He is intellectually, but if we do not enter into communion with Him on a personal level and allow this union to impact our everyday lives we essentially only know "about" Jesus and do not "know" Him. The same holds true with Mary.

THE MOST BLESSED SACRAMENT
The Holy Eucharist

Another great sticking point for non-Catholics is the doctrine about the Eucharist. So much can be said about the Holy Eucharist—the Real Presence of Jesus Christ in Holy Communion, the Blessed Sacrament—that I am inadequate to do it justice. After all, it is the actual Body, Blood, Soul, and Divinity of our Lord and Savior Jesus Christ truly present in the elements of bread and wine. It is the source and summit of the entire Catholic faith. By this time in my faith journey, my heart was opening wider and wider to the truths of Catholicism, and as a result it was easier for me to grasp new doctrines and teachings that I never knew growing up in a Protestant church. Everything, I found, that the Catholic Church teaches is interconnected in one form or another. Like a giant web, it was all one. When it came time to study the Holy Eucharist I felt a specific drawing to It. The one thing I desired most out of all of this study was to draw closer to our Lord, the One who gave me a second chance at life. I wanted to cling to Him as close as I could. I knew that He contained the life that my soul, and everyone else's soul, longed for. My heart was beating for intimacy with Him, my Creator, and He was drawing me closer to this end.

The idea of Jesus Christ being truly present in Holy Communion was revolutionary to me. It seemed to me that it is either simply too good to be true or it is downright an abomination or idolatry. I saw no in-between. To be able to say, "There is Jesus!" at every Catholic Mass as the very people did when they saw Jesus incarnate some 2,000 years ago mesmerized me. It seemed to me that this would make anyone's walk of faith in Christ come alive one hundred fold. It was one extreme or another; either Jesus' words in the Gospels, "this is my body" and "this is my blood," were in fact true or they weren't. To me, this is what separates Catholicism from all other Christian faith traditions. These words of our Lord and how Christians have understood them throughout the history of Christianity made a world of difference in my own life as a Christian. By this time, however, our Lord had already placed a longing in my heart to receive Him in this Blessed Sacrament. It contained within it all sweetness and power, strength and love.

I recalled watching Holy Mass on Catholic television and being captivated by the prayers said during the Liturgy of the Eucharist. They were so beautiful and they contained something so deep the likes of which I had never heard before. The way in which the priest, and the laity, showed reverence toward Holy Communion spoke volumes to the witness of the Real Presence of Jesus Christ. Watching, like I had seen earlier on the same station, adoration of the Blessed Sacrament on television with the friars also told me that there was something unique about what Catholics believed in Holy Communion. After all, why would they be treating something that seemed to be a piece of mere bread and some wine in such a way if it did not have the significance it really had? They would be utter fools, and they would look absolutely ridiculous! This took tremendous faith on their part, and the fruits of their lives bore witness again to what they believed. This, also, is a testimony for all of us, that when we live out our faith in true authenticity it will attract people.

Almost from the start of my studies on the Holy Eucharist I knew I had already been convinced of its reality and truth, at least from an intellectual perspective. God, being the gentleman that He is, took it one step further. A good friend of mine and his family decided to go to a traditional Latin Mass one Sunday at a parish nearby. There were only a few parishes within our archdiocese that offered the old Tridentine or Latin Mass, and we found one. I remember the day well, because it was the Sunday after Pope John Paul II had died. The Mass itself was held in a parish that looked as if it had been brought straight out of the Middle

Ages. It was gothic and didn't look anything like most of the other Catholic parishes I was familiar with. This was the first time I stepped foot inside of a Catholic Church since we had to visit one when I was in catechism class in the Lutheran church some 20 years prior. Even then, I do not recall anything special about it. At that time I wasn't interested in learning about my faith, so it pretty much meant nothing to me. Now, it meant everything to me! As I entered the nave, the silence was the first thing I noticed. There was a sense of real holiness unlike anything I had ever witnessed before. As the Holy Mass started, it differed a bit from the Mass I watched on television in regard to the language and the form. This Holy Mass saw the priest facing the altar with his back toward the people. The Mass I watched on television saw the priest the other way around, facing the people. I wasn't quite sure at that time what exactly was happening, and it was difficult to follow the Mass because it was said entirely in Latin. Nevertheless, I carefully watched the people around me and followed their lead as to when to stand up, sit down, kneel, etc. It was interesting watching what was happening around me and at the altar, and despite not knowing what was said, I felt—I knew—something extraordinary was occurring.

When the time came for the Liturgy of the Eucharist, something happened that forever changed my life and my view of Jesus Christ and Christianity. As we were kneeling during the consecration, the priest elevated the Sacred Host and immediately I was struck with the same overwhelming presence of almighty God that I had the moment in which He miraculously healed me of alcoholism! I almost fell back into my seat; the presence of Jesus was so strong! It was as if the heavens were opened for me and God the Father proclaimed, "Behold, my Son!" I felt pure holiness before me. It was one of those instances when one who is sensitive to the Spirit of God would pause and say, "...He's here!" By this event God had shown to me not only intellectually that Jesus is truly present in the Eucharist, but He confirmed this in my heart. This, I thought, is what I've been searching for! Ever since I was delivered from alcohol addiction the Lord had placed in my heart a desire to know Him intimately. How much more intimate can you get than to have Him, my savior, my deliverer, and my God, dwell within me not only spiritually but physically as well! I wasn't able to receive Him at the time, but my heart longed to.

8

Glory Revisited

Glorious, King!

You alone know the desires of our hearts!

Lead us all to the place of pure delight,

Your Sacred Heart!

The incident at the Latin Mass was the final straw. It was pretty much the confirmation I needed to know that God was calling me into the Catholic Church. I knew it was going to be a very difficult path, but one I knew I needed to follow if I wanted to remain obedient to Him. I knew it could result in a lot of division among my fellow non-Catholic Christian friends and family and myself. Since the Catholic Church is viewed by many non-Catholics as heretical and even non-Christian to some, I knew that it was going to take nothing short of an act of God to show them what was happening and why I was being called into this Church. At this time I sought all things Catholic: books, radio, television, etc. I didn't personally know any practicing Catholics either. Sadly, the Catholics I did know weren't practicing their faith, so as a result even if I were to try to seek their help they wouldn't understand the significance of what was happening. I needed someone who knew what I was talking about. From everything I've studied to everything the Lord had revealed to me, I needed someone to give me direction and a helping hand in finding out exactly how I could come into the Church. I had no idea what the process was. With Protestantism, all one would have to do is simply align his or her beliefs with that of the particular church and begin going to Sunday service! That's all! This wasn't the case with Catholicism, however. I knew at this point that my baptism in the Lutheran Church was valid in the Catholic Church because it was done the same way in which the Church, who is the voice of God, prescribed it to be done according to the teachings of Jesus Himself and His disciples and Sacred Tradition. I just needed to be confirmed into the Church, but did not know how to go about it.

By the grace of God this is when I met Abel. Abel is a devoted, practicing Catholic I met online while researching Catholic material. We quickly developed a friendship and Abel was patient enough to answer some of the more difficult questions I had concerning Catholic teaching. He walked me through beliefs such as Purgatory, indulgences, statues, and icons, pointing me to the source of what the Church really teaches about such tough doctrines and why they teach it. I am forever grateful to Abel for his authentic Catholic witness.

I had tried to contact some local priests to talk with them but to no avail. They never returned my phone calls or e-mails. It began to get frustrating after a while, since my heart was longing for the Holy Eucharist and I knew I couldn't receive Him just yet because I hadn't been received into the Church. I even stopped going to Holy Mass for a while because it was too difficult to watch others receive the Lord in the Blessed Sacrament while I had to simply watch. So at this point I wasn't going to Mass and I couldn't go to a non-Catholic Church in good conscience either. What made matters worse was I didn't tell everyone about this calling yet either. It was difficult for me to explain, knowing the opposition I would face. Yet at the same time most of my family and friends knew I was heading in this direction. I was quoting saints, reading Catholic books, and talking Catholic as far as my beliefs. In fact, a few friends had pulled me aside and spoke to me about their concern. I understood Catholicism, but there was still something in them that was resistant to my story; no matter what was said, they didn't "get it." I had to constantly question myself as to whether or not this was indeed where I believe God was calling me. But there was no mistaking. I knew, almost as a couple simply knows that they are to marry. It was based not only on intellectual truths but on a deep and unmistakable love for Jesus Christ. I desired the most of Him wherever I could find it. What my soul longed for was the Catholic Church, the fullness of the Christian faith, who exercises every detail of what Christ desired to give us, that help us lead holy lives that end with the Beatific Vision. It had answered all of my questions and cleared away any doubt and confusion. Now was the time to act!

Late one Sunday evening I was flipping through the TV stations when I came across a television show on a local station. The show was called, "The One True Faith." It caught my attention with such a blunt title and I decided to watch part of it just to see what "their" version of the "true faith" was. However, lo and behold, I was blown away because the very things that they were talking about were the very things that I had been studying! It was no-nonsense Catholicism! I couldn't believe it! Once the show ended I quickly wrote down the show's information and found out that it was a local show filmed right here in the Detroit area! I wasted no time in contacting them. I wrote them an e-mail the following day describing my situation and all that the Lord had done and brought me through. To be honest I really didn't think I would receive a response, but as God would have it they responded almost immediately! I was floored! The hand of God was clearly moving again. We set up a meeting where I could visit the studio and speak with them in hopes that they could shed some light on how I could finally get into the Church.

It was wonderful! I met and spoke with the producer and it was a huge sigh of relief on my part because it was the first time I spoke with someone in person who actually understood what I was talking about! He invited me to Holy Mass the following Sunday and said he would introduce me to the priest and then see what the next step would be. Oddly enough, the parish in which we were to attend Mass was the same parish where I had my profound encounter with Jesus in the Blessed Sacrament! I knew God was opening avenues and pointing me in the right direction. When Sunday came, we met at the parish and attended Mass, and I was then invited to a talk that the host of the show "The One True Faith" was going to give to the Knights of Columbus. It was at this time that I met Father and we spoke briefly about my story. He responded enthusiastically about my willingness to come into the Church. He told me to call his office on Monday to set something up.

So Monday came and I called his office to speak with him but he wasn't available. *No problem*, I thought, *I'll just try later.* So I called later in the day and the same thing happened—he wasn't available. So I left a message with the secretary in hopes that he would respond within a day or two. Day after day passed and I heard nothing. I sent him an e-mail requesting to speak with him and again, after waiting several days, nothing. What was going on here? *This was strange*, I thought. *Why would he sound so willing to meet and then give me the cold shoulder?* I shook it off as him being too busy and I was anxious to get things moving, so I proceeded to other avenues.

I e-mailed several priests in the area and told each of them my situation and even with this none of them responded! Once again I began questioning myself as to whether or not this was the right path our Lord wanted me to follow. It was very difficult for me to understand the Lord's ways and how He goes about accomplishing certain things. Why was it seemingly so simple for me to recognize the "signs" our Lord was showing me while discerning if He was calling me in the Catholic Church, yet difficult to actually get into the Church?

By this time it was Advent and I went to the Midnight Mass at the Cathedral with a friend and her family to celebrate the Lord's birth with the archbishop. The mother of my friend knew one of the monsignors who were concelebrating this Holy Mass and she was to introduce me to him afterward. Once Holy Mass ended we met the archbishop (which was the first time I met him or any archbishop) and we then spoke to the monsignor. Briefly, I told him my story and he seemed delighted to offer me any assistance I needed to finally be able to be fully received into the Church.

However, once again I waited and waited and heard nothing in response. By this time I was so discouraged I honestly thought I would never get in unless God Himself performed a miracle. Why was God putting up this much resistance between me and my ful-filling His call to enter into His Church? I would only later find out, but for now I thought that there was no reason why it should be this hard. All that I needed was some support and someone to simply tell me where I needed to go and what I needed to do.

I recall attending Holy Mass one specific evening at this time, and after Mass had ended I stayed in the pew and prayed. Little by little the people left and I was one of maybe three or four people left in the entire church. It had been an evening Mass and it was dark outside, and the ushers had already dimmed the lights in the main part of the church. I then walked over to the Shrine of Jesus, which stood to the back of the nave, and lit one of many candles signifying the continued prayers of us on earth rising to heaven before the throne of the Lamb of God. I knelt down before the statue of our Lord and prayed in tears that He might open up a door to make it easy for me to come into His fold. I begged Him, leaving nothing out. I left that evening feeling confident that Christ heard my prayers and I placed my complete trust in His Divine Providence.

After not too many days had passed, I was listening to a powerful local priest preach/talk on Catholic radio. The show itself wasn't a live radio talk show, but recordings of talks which he had given—very thought-provoking talks which pitted current social issues and daily living against authentic Catholic teaching. Even though I had been listening to Father's talks for a while now, it never dawned on me to contact him. Perhaps because I figured he was a "Catholic celebrity" of sorts and most likely didn't have the time to respond to someone like me. However, I decided one day, after all else had seemed to fail, to write him an e-mail. To be honest, I wasn't expecting anything in return, but I thought I would write and hope that maybe, just maybe, he would answer me. After a couple of days had passed I noticed that, by the grace of God, he **did** answer me! I had initially written an e-mail asking whether he could suggest any priests in my area (his parish was about an hour away) who would be willing to talk with me about coming into the Church. Surprisingly, he didn't. But he did invite me to come and speak with him in person and try to work something out.

I was a bit hesitant at first, considering the circumstances. It might seem odd, but with little to no support from family and friends this was a very difficult step of faith for me—especially after not being able to contact and actually talk to any priest after several attempts. I was a bit discouraged. As a result, he and I spoke a few more times via e-mail, and I finally got the nerve to set up an appointment. By this time it was already winter and the season of

Lent was quickly approaching. After Lent came the Easter Vigil, which, generally speaking, is the normal time when adults are fully received into the Church. I was hoping that since I pretty much already knew the Catholic faith from all the studying I had done on my own, I wouldn't have to attend the regular RCIA (Rite of Catholic Initiation for Adults) classes and wait until the Easter Vigil, which was still a few months away. I was ready for the Eucharist now! I wanted to be united to Christ so badly that I even missed Holy Mass on a few occasions because it was simply too hard for me to not receive our Lord in the Blessed Sacrament while attending. At any rate, I desired any way in which God Himself saw fit for me to come in. RCIA or not, I was ready.

This visit turned out not only to be an answer to prayer but a pivotal turning point in my journey. The appointment was about a month from the time I had called to set it up, because he was a very busy man. The anticipation building in my heart, fully knowing that God was behind this, was unbelievable. THIS, I knew, was it! I was finally going to get some answers and be able to move forward. So after work I drove the hour it took to get there and spoke with him face to face. I knew I only had about an hour to explain my entire journey of faith and get his advice. I told him my story from birth, my alcohol addiction, my miraculous deliverance, and everything since then that had led me to where I was speaking with him that day. Father sat patiently and listened intently as I explained where God had led me. I fully understood that once I was received into the Catholic Church God would then begin to work in my life as never before, almost as if He were fitting me with the armor of God and the remaining pieces I needed to put on could only be found in the Catholic Church.

After I had finished talking, with a rather puzzled look on his face, Father said, "Why aren't you in the Church yet?" It was almost as if God were asking me why I was so reluctant. I really didn't have an adequate answer to give him. Why *wasn't* I in the Church yet? Any answer I gave only served as an excuse, because I knew all too well that I should've been a lot more persistent knowing that this is indeed where God Himself was calling me. I came face to face with the fact that I didn't trust God. I never told this to Father, but I immediately thought it; I immediately knew it to be true. He then quoted the words of Christ, as if Jesus Himself were saying them to me. "For whoever is ashamed of me and my words, of him will the Son of Man be ashamed when He comes in His glory and the glory of the Father and of the holy angels" (Luke 9:26). At long last, this was the final push it took for me. God had now not only shown me why it was taking so long, but He also revealed to me the stubbornness of my own heart as relates to obedience. I knew full well that some people would oppose my obedience to Christ to follow Him into the Catholic Church, especially my closest family and friends. I had to step up in faith and not be ashamed of Christ in His Church, and look beyond my fears of causing anyone sorrow or pain by becoming a Catholic. I had to trust God, once again, that He knows what He's doing and that He is in control of my life and not me. He would take care of my loved ones and I needed to take care of myself and my own obedience to Him.

Father expressed his desire for me to join his parish but saw it more practical that I attend a parish closer to my home. He recommended a certain parish nearby (the one, ironically, that I was attending already) and told me to contact the priest, whom he knew would take care of me. The very next day I e-mailed the priest, and he responded the same day! He suggested I visit the RCIA group and see what I thought. I wanted to get into the Church as soon as I possibly could, but in obedience to Christ's representative on earth, I agreed with much enthusiasm. I contacted the RCIA director and explained the situation, and was invited to attend the next class.

I was on fire once again! I was so eager to meet everyone and finally get things rolling. Everyone in the RCIA class, teachers and students, were unbelievably supportive. It was now February and the rest of the students had been attending class since the fall, and I felt somewhat awkward having come in when the class was almost over. Nevertheless, they were all very kind and welcoming. The fellowship was great as I was finally among those who were in the same boat as I was. They understood what I had been teaching myself the past four or five years, and that was a great comfort to me.

Not only was I learning more and meeting a lot of amazing people, but I also had the privilege of participating in the Holy Mass in a new way. It may not seem like a big deal to most Catholics, but to me to bring up the gifts before the Eucharist (the sacred vessels used during the Liturgy of the Eucharist and the unconsecrated bread and wine) was one of the greatest honors ever bestowed on me. Also special to me were the rites in which we catechumens were able to participate during the process of coming into the Church. Being able to go to the cathedral before the archbishop himself and have our names called and enrolled in the Church in the beautiful Rite of Election was utterly breathtaking. Just being part of this ancient Christian tradition was amazing, knowing that this was what Christians have been doing for centuries. Everything had meaning and purpose. Nothing was done carelessly, because this was the most important decision anyone could make in his or her entire life. It held eternal weight, and God Himself judged our hearts as we declared our willingness to come before Him. The time had come that I had been waiting for. I was ready to be confirmed into the One, Holy, Catholic, and Apostolic Church!

In the process of being fully received into the Catholic Church, one of the steps is to go to confession before receiving confirmation. This is mandatory (for those who were previously baptized), as one needs to be in a state of grace in order to receive confirmation and the Holy Eucharist. Never having been to confession before, I simply longed for this day! I saw the tremendous grace involved and knew that the priest stood in persona Christi, or, in English, stood "in the person of Christ" when hearing confessions. However, this was a challenge for me as well. I was 32 years old and had to do an examination of conscience that spanned my entire life up to that point. I had plenty of time to prepare and I knew what I had to do. I admit that having to dig up some of the more shameful aspects of my past and tell them to someone (a priest no less) wasn't a pleasant thought. Nevertheless, Christ gave me the grace to do so.

I was to be confirmed at the Easter Vigil, which took place on the Saturday before Easter. We had our confession on the previous Wednesday evening. I was eagerly anticipating this event because I knew, without a doubt, Jesus awaited and I knew He would meet me in a powerful way. On the drive there I almost ended up in a car accident. I had driven the same route to my parish many times before and had never encountered such an instance. I was driving about 35-40 mph around a curve in the road where you cannot fully see who is in front of you but for maybe 20-30 yards. As I was turning, the car in front of me had fully stopped to make a left turn. I didn't see him until I was already halfway around the curve. So I had to slam on the brakes and swerve onto the shoulder to avoid hitting him. Fortunately, the roads weren't wet or slick and no one was behind or in front of me, so I managed to avoid a possible wreck. Afterward, I thought to myself how odd it would've been to be in a car accident on the way to my very first confession! A coincidence—you tell me?

All of us from the RCIA group met in the small chapel where the confessionals are and listened to a brief sermon by the deacon on the power of confession. We were once again reminded of what words we are to say; i.e., bless me Father, for I have sinned.... We were all nervous but at the same time we were in eager anticipation of what might be a life-changing moment. The presence of God, at least to me, was overwhelming. One by one we entered the confessional. Tears were streaming down the faces of many because the mercy of almighty God had pierced their hearts. It was now my turn. Upon entering the confessional I saw the option of either kneeling behind a curtain and confessing or sitting face-to-face with the priest (in persona Christi). I chose the latter because I felt it would add to the effectiveness of my confession.

Since this was my first confession I wrote everything down on a piece of paper because, unfortunately, there was so much garbage I had to unload. I was literally shaking in the confessional because this was a very difficult thing for me to do. Nevertheless, the grace of almighty God showered upon me and I was able to finish with a clear conscience. I had confessed everything that I could honestly remember. Father then offered some practical advice and even added, "I can see that you did your homework!" He then said the most beautiful words anyone can hear: the words of absolution. At once I felt the power and mercy of God surge through me and burn away my sins like wheat. I was forgiven of everything! The burden and subsequent relief was absolutely incredible! I had the sense that God was waiting for this moment: a Father longing for the opportunity to forgive His child. I could now understand how, like Jesus told St. Faustina, God's mercy is far, far greater than any of our sins. I understood that absolutely nothing we could do to offend God is beyond His ability to forgive us. The greatest aspect, I believe, is God's sheer willingness to forgive us!

I left the confessional with a smile on my face. I felt incredible as I realized that I really was going to be a Catholic! This was truly where Jesus was calling me. I hadn't felt that alive in such a long time. I couldn't wait until the Easter Vigil. I could see how God was slowly placing each piece of His armor upon me one by one and equipping me to finally be able to do battle for Him and help save souls. I could understand the necessity of each sacrament and the grace with which it infuses us. We absolutely need them in order to be all that Christ is calling us to be. It was almost as if I were climbing a mountain and the summit was the Eucharist. I was almost there!

It was a windy, cool day in early April when I headed up to my parish for the Easter Vigil. I had never been to a vigil before, and so not only was this the very day God would seal me with the gift of the Holy Spirit through the Sacrament of Confirmation, but I would be able to experience the very pinnacle of the Church year as we rejoice in the resurrection of our Lord Jesus Christ! None of my family members or non-Catholic friends attended (although my mother expressed her desire to be there but was unable to), but just my sponsor, his wife, my good friend Abel, and another good friend, Lauryn, and her family. We stood outside listening intently to Father pray the blessing over the fire which would light the traditional Easter candle, which represented the light of Christ in the world. I stood as close as I could; the anticipation was building. This, I thought, is it! It is really happening! We paraded inside the church chanting praises to God the entire time for His infinite goodness and glory. We were seated in the very first row and the rest of the Holy Mass seemed surreal.

After the Scripture readings, those ready to be baptized were asked to approach the baptismal font in the center aisle as we all chanted the beautiful Litany of the Saints. All of us who were not being baptized stood nearby and supported those being baptized with our prayers. One by one, four catechumens were baptized in the name of the Father, Son, and Holy Spirit, thus cleansing them of all original sin and personal sins and placing them into the Body of Christ. It was incredible to witness this firsthand, as I had never witnessed a Catholic baptism before. The prayers said were unspeakably powerful and profound. This was another instance that overwhelmed me to tears, since this was the very thing that Catholic Christians have been doing for centuries. All of heaven was looking down and welcoming these new souls who made a decision for Jesus Christ.

After this the priest called us to gather in front of the altar. All of us had the name of our confirmation patron saint upon our chests. He called us up one by one, and I will never forget this moment. It was the culmination of my life up to this point. It was the very thing God wanted me to do in order to be fully prepared to embrace what He was calling me to do and to lead the life He intended me to live. Under normal circumstances it is the bishop who confirms the faithful, but at the Easter Vigil, since there are so many catechumens around the archdiocese, the archbishop allows the parish priests to confirm us. With the Sacred Chrism in hand, Father called me up to the altar first. "St. Polycarp" he said, "I sign thee with the sign of the cross, and I confirm thee with the chrism of salvation, in the name of the Father and of the Son and of the Holy Ghost." He then placed his hand on the side of my face and welcomed me as the newest Catholic.

Not only was my confirmation my official entrance into the Catholic Church, but it was the very first time I would be able to receive our Precious Lord, Jesus Christ, in the Holy Eucharist! Being seated in the first row, I had an up-close encounter with Jesus as the priest consecrated the elements. It was incredible! As the priest said the Eucharistic Prayer, I felt myself being pulled toward Christ in a way that I never experienced before. It was a unity of love unlike any other known to man that connected my entire heart, mind, and soul with that of its Creator. We then went up and knelt before the altar where the sacrifice was made and I heard the most beautiful words said as I prepared myself to receive my Lord sacramentally, "The Body and Blood of Christ." The priest dipped the Sacred Host in the Precious Blood (a form of communion called intinction) and I obediently consumed my Lord Jesus Christ in complete Body, Blood, Soul, and Divinity for the very first time.

I was told a day or so before my confirmation that we can ask one thing of Jesus upon receiving Him in the Blessed Sacrament for the very first time and He would grant it. Not given too long to think about it, I prayed for the one thing I knew would help my cause. I prayed that the Lord would grant me a holy boldness to proclaim His Gospel without fear. I understood that I would need the boldness I saw in the holy martyrs I had read about, the saints throughout the ages who all had to stand up to opposition but nevertheless proclaimed the Good News of Jesus Christ proudly and with confidence! That's what I longed for and that is what I asked our Lord to grant me upon receiving Him for the first time.

After I consumed the Holy Eucharist I wasn't brought into a state of ecstasy or given any sublime revelation, but I was filled with a sense of fulfillment. A feeling of completeness shrouded me and I knew I was home.

Once Holy Mass had ended, a large Host was placed in the monstrance and Christ was led around the sanctuary for adoration. I found myself once again uniquely drawn to Him. Where the priest went, whether it was in front of me, beside me, or in back of me, I found my body turning in the direction in which He was led. With head bowed in worship, I was being "wooed" by my Lord and I strongly desired to be where He was. It was one of those moments when you can say with conviction, "He is here!" I felt like one of the disciples as I was enraptured in His Eucharistic glory! I had *finally* arrived! And this was only the beginning!

Just like the day our Lord completely healed me of my alcohol addiction and I had the words, "Glory, glory, glory" swarming around in my head, I experienced the same thing when coming into the Catholic Church! I felt on top of the world; I felt utterly invincible! I was home now. There is nothing greater in this life than knowing you are doing the will of almighty God! I knew that this is exactly where He wanted me to be. I was so in love with Him that it's difficult to write down all that was happening inside of me. Unlike my deliverance from alcohol and coming back to the Lord, when I had to get to know Him, I already *knew* Him this time, and it was as if we were now fully made one, my soul and His. He resided within me, not only spiritually, but physically as well, through the Holy Eucharist. That's true intimacy, and what a gift it is! Once a soul understands exactly Whom it is he is receiving in the Sacrament of the Altar, he is never again the same. It was all that my soul was longing for and now it came to fruition. I knew, however, that a lot of work still needed to be done within the kingdom of God, but now I was fully equipped to take on whatever our Most Merciful Lord sends my way.

I want to take the time now to mention a very valued friend, a sincere brother in the faith, and probably the only one who had been supporting me, strengthening me, and encouraging me throughout my *entire* journey into the Church. From the time I picked up my very first Catholic book until my confirmation into the Church, Abel Ruiz had walked with me through thick and thin. Being a lifelong Catholic himself and having reverted back to the faith, he patiently answered all my questions and walked me through some of the tougher Catholic doctrines when needed. Abel would faithfully research difficult questions I had and give me very educated, truthful answers. Despite living at opposite ends of the country, we were able to connect via e-mail and we would correspond regularly. In fact, I met Abel for the first time at my confirmation. I cannot thank him enough for all that he has done for me in guiding me in the right direction.

Glory be to the Father, and to the Son, and to the Holy Spirit. As it was in the beginning, is now, and ever shall be, world without end, AMEN.

9

A New Voice for Broken Souls

Jesus, Redeemer and Lord, my life is Yours.

Lead me where You may...

Pope Benedict XVI wrote in his encyclical letter *Deus Caritas Est* (*God Is Love*):

> *"Being Christian is not the result of an ethical choice or a lofty idea, but the encounter with an event, a person, which gives life a new horizon and a decisive direction."* (Paragraph 1)

What God has brought me through is only the beginning of what He has in store for me. But this book, this story, is not only about me. It's about the love, the mercy, the grace, and the compassion of the Blessed Trinity. I write this as a means to not only proclaim that God is still active and performing miracles in our day, but that no matter what circumstances you or someone you may know and love are in, there is always hope. I have been to the brink of utter despair. I know what it is like to know that you're dying. I have felt the chains of addiction and the violent cycle of sin that accompanies it. I know what it is like to lose everything and lose all hope in humanity and one's self. I know that the only place to turn is to turn toward heaven. God is misunderstood by so many! I, too, in the midst of my chaos believed that God was angry with me and was peering down upon my black soul just waiting for me to die so He could cast me into hell where I deserved to be. I lost hope that there was any way I could please Him. This, perhaps, was my greatest misery.

Even though I lost hope in everything, including God, He never lost hope in me. I was not seeking Him or even asking Him for anything, because I was convinced that there was no way He would help me due to what I had done with my life. What I quickly found out, however, was that God is not like that. Even though I didn't believe it at the time, His love for me—and for every one of us—is so unfathomable that it completely transcends our own understanding. What we need to understand, and what I came to know, is that there is absolutely nothing we ourselves can do to merit His grace and love. He knows we're helpless. His hope is that we do not wait until we hit the bottom before we turn to Him. God has created all of us to naturally long for Him and to unite ourselves with Him. By this, we are satisfied. I was never taught this growing up. I naturally thought our happiness lies in what we ourselves believe will make us happy. For me, what I thought would make me happy would have killed me, had not God stepped in!

Even more than hope, perhaps, my story is a story about love. Once I found what my heart has always been longing for, I yearned to know more about the source from which it came. All of my efforts, all of my prayers, all of my studies, and all of my tears were geared toward becoming one with the One who gave me my life and gave me back my life. It was from Him I gained it and it was from Him I lost it and received it once again. If God had not allowed me to experience all these things, I wouldn't be the person whom He wanted me to be today. As bad as my life had become, by His mercy He still used it for my greater good.

Is this a reason to continue living a life in sin? Of course not! What I recognized is that the love that God poured onto me, I in turn was to pour out on others. How, then, could I pour out this divine love onto others if I do not have access to the grace that He gives to enable us? It was for this very reason Jesus gave us the sacraments. The sacraments are an outward sign of an inward grace given to our souls. Therefore, with the sacraments, not only did I find a way to be fully united with God, who gave me a second chance at life, but I would have the grace to love others with the same love He gives to me.

Christianity seemed to me at one point just an aspect of life. There were, I believed, different areas of life that were simply meant to be kept separate, i.e., our family life, our jobs, our friends, and so forth. Religion was to be kept as something personal, not to influence us in our other relationships. I saw no harm in it, but religion was to be kept by itself as just an aspect of what someone might personally believe, but it would never influence the other areas of his or her life.

What I discovered, however, is the opposite. God, in His unfathomable love for us, shows us how we can live a life of satisfaction and authentic happiness throughout every aspect of our lives—with ourselves, first of all, and with our family, friends, co-workers, etc. Since, therefore, He is the author of life, our Creator, and the source of eternal joy, He alone knows what will make us happy. I didn't believe this but once I was forced into a corner by my own doing, God in His mercy revealed this truth to me in a way that I could never have imagined.

This divine reality is for everyone, not just for certain people. It's not about being "good enough" to earn God's love. It's about trusting Him that there is far more to life than what we see. When you ask God with a contrite heart and in humility, He will stretch forth His arms and embrace you wherever you're at and reveal

Himself to you. We must understand that we need to meet God on His terms and not our own. We cannot have a preconceived idea of how God works and how He conducts Himself within the affairs of humanity. We need to know that we are to meet Him in the way He has divinely revealed Himself to us: through His Church and through His Living Word, Sacred Scripture, which are one and the same. The new voice I have is not of human origin, but eternal. It is a voice that knows that this life on earth is not what we were created for. It is a voice which carries with it hope, love, happiness, and peace.

I cannot promise you that God will perform a miracle in your own life as He did in mine or in the lives of those whom you love, but what I can tell you, with certainty and with conviction, is that He alone knows you better than you know yourself. He alone knows what is the absolute best for you in your life. If you sincerely and honestly surrender your will to know, love, and serve Him, then He will, in love, meet you where you're at and transform your life. Behold, He stands knocking at the door of your heart. Do not postpone His beckoning, for you never know when your life will be required of you. He loves you more than anyone else ever will or can, and all He asks is that you love Him in return.

I want to encourage those who have already willingly received the love of almighty God and who walk with Him to realize the tremendous witness you have in the lives of those around you. Throughout the entire time I was drinking, when things took a turn for the worse and I had nowhere to turn, my aunt stepped out in faith and witnessed to me the mercy and love that God had for me. No one else up to that point had done so, and that was the very thing I needed to hear. Even though at the time I never could've dreamed of the actual impact it would have in my life, it was nevertheless the stepping-stone, the seed planted, that ended up sprouting into a new creation.

We have been given such a gift. We cannot fail to underestimate the power we have been given. We cannot be fearful or ashamed to spread the Good News of Jesus Christ. Lives depend on our witness. If we would all step out in faith with boldness, conviction, and trust in the Almighty, life-changing power of God, the world would be turned upside down! We are all called to be witnesses to the love and mercy of Jesus Christ by the very lives we lead. In fact, the word "witness" used in the Greek appropriate to this calling is "martys" which is literally translated as "martyr." It's defined as, "Those who after His example have proved the strength and genuineness of their faith in Christ by undergoing a violent death" (*Strong's Exhaustive Concordance of the Bible*, #G3144).

We may not all be called to martyrdom in the literal sense, but we absolutely must have the complete abandonment within ourselves that if Christ is calling us to such, we must be ready and willing. The martyrdom to which the majority of today's Christians are called is referred to as a White Martyrdom (Red Martyrdom being to physically die for Christ), where the persecutions of modern society can, and usually are, a hindrance to our persevering in faith. It might be the fear of ridicule, or the daily struggle to die to self and loose the bonds of inordinate attachments to worldly things.

Whatever witness we are called to by our Lord Jesus Christ, we must realize that it is of the utmost importance that we comply. Therefore, I urge all Christians who read this to *please* step out in faith like my aunt did for me, and never be afraid to approach someone you know who is struggling with an addiction or suffering in another way with the loving, tender mercy of Jesus Christ. Be a witness, be a martyr, empty yourself for the sake of another and be Christ Jesus to someone who is in dire need of Him.

Find your inspiration in those spiritual masters of years past, the saints. Learn from them how to deal with difficult problems and overcome them through Christ. I cannot stress enough the inestimable value of the Communion of Saints within the Catholic Church. God calls each and every one of us to be saints and has given us the means by which to achieve this. The rest is up to us. Living a life of heroic virtue in our day and age is something most wanting. We will stand out as a sore thumb among the crowds, but it will be a life lived pleasing to God and with eternal happiness forever with the God of gods and Lord of lords as our reward. Surrender, therefore, and remember always the very first words of Blessed Pope John Paul II upon his elevation to the papacy: "Be not afraid!!"

Acknowledgements

This book and my entire life is the result of the immeasurable love of the Most Blessed Trinity who gave me a second chance at life—without whom neither myself nor this book would be here.

I humbly thank Michele Bondi Bottesi who cooperated with Divine Providence and saw potential in my story and encouraged me to write it. Her unceasing help, advice, support, encouragement and most of all her prayers have been a true testimony to the love of Jesus Christ and His Church.

With a most sincere and grateful heart I wish to thank John-Paul and Nancy Belanger for copy-editing my story and also for all of their prayers and support. God will certainly reward you for your efforts.

I thank Erin Howarth as well for her expertise and suggestions in the book layout and design. Your helpful advice and suggestions have been very appreciated.

In addition I want to thank the following people for their support in making my book possible: Bill and Janet Mackinnon, Father Ben Kosnac, Sheryl Pantti McGeary, Nikkie Kurkules and the many others who have contributed to making this book possible.